## Camping's Fun Until...

Your buddy's chopping wood and suddenly can't move his arm! Your wife steps on a twig and discovers it's a snake that bites! Your son's feeding nuts to a squirrel and it sinks its teeth into his hand! Pain stabs at your abdomen when you're miles from a hospital!

If you must doctor on your own, turn to the Problem-Treatment-Finder in this manual. It directs you from symptoms to diagnosis, diagrams emergency surgical and bone-setting methods, suggests medicines, and prevents you from making dangerous treatment mistakes. Take along *Being Your Own Wilderness Doctor* when you vacation; it's an Rx for peace of mind.

**Being Your Own Wilderness Doctor**
was originally published by
Stackpole Books.

# THE OUTDOORSMAN'S EMERGENCY MANUAL

# BEING YOUR OWN WILDERNESS DOCTOR

Dr. E. Russel Kodet
and Bradford Angier

PUBLISHED BY POCKET BOOKS NEW YORK

BEING YOUR OWN WILDERNESS DOCTOR

Stackpole edition published March, 1968
POCKET BOOK edition published May, 1972
3rd printing...........June, 1972

This POCKET BOOK edition includes every word
contained in the original, higher-priced edition. It is printed
from brand-new plates made from completely reset, clear, easy-to-read
type. POCKET BOOK editions are published by POCKET BOOKS, a division
of Simon & Schuster, Inc., 630 Fifth Avenue, New York, N.Y. 10020.
Trademarks registered in the United States and other countries.

L

Standard Book Number: 671-78549-4.
Library of Congress Catalog Card Number: 68-15440.

*For Shirley and for Vena*

# CONTENTS

[ 7 ]

# PROBLEM-TREATMENT-FINDER

[ 9 ]

# BEING YOUR OWN
# WILDERNESS
# DOCTOR

# 1

## MORE THAN MERELY
## FIRST AID

THIS BOOK is intended as a reference for those who may venture into the back regions—places in which ready access to professional medical help would be impossible or unusually time-consuming because of a region's geography and sparse population. This is *not* a home reference for the health problems of everyday life or a treatment substitute for those traveling or living where physicians and medical facilities are readily available.

Even though you should decide against undertaking the kind of doctoring that might seem needed in an emergency while in a far-away place, this book tells how a physician would see the problem. This could enable you to make a correct and possibly life-saving decision at a critical time.

The decision might require turning back for

medical help at once or, failing that, staying where you are and signaling for help. On the other hand, you might gain a sense of relief through learning that what seems a formidable health problem really isn't that serious. It might prove a very temporary one, some minor thing that needn't disrupt all plans.

Also, this book might prevent you from doing something stupid in an emergency—there are occasions when it's tough and even terrifying to be the one who has to decide what to do and to assume all of the responsibility. That's when *not knowing* what ought to be done hurts. And bad decisions—made in ignorance—are truly sometimes the hardest kinds to outlive.

Through the miracle of modern forms of transportation it is easily possible today to visit relatively remote regions, even on a weekend. If you love visiting the back lands, follow good general rules. The outdoorsman having a special health problem such as diabetes or epilepsy, etc., should always get complete counsel from his doctor before heading for the remote reaches.

No book of this kind could possibly handle diabetes, gout, asthma, and similar problems since these and many other disorders are highly technical. Fortunately, with asthma and many other chronic problems, the patient usually is conscious. Frequently he is sufficiently familiar with the needed proper treatment to be able to direct it himself.

Attend carefully to the differences between problems absolutely requiring professional help and those which you may undertake in camp or on the trail when medical help is not available. Appendicitis and some other conditions, of course, will require a surgeon. There is a way, nevertheless, by which you can distinguish between an acute abdomen, a case where one certainly must have professional help, or a case of simple colic or lesser disturbance. Watch carefully therefore for various symptomatic distinctions and always seek medical help when it's available.

This book suggests the kinds and quantities of medicines that are most often useful or needed for back-country outings. It recommends that you consult your doctor for assistance in making up the supply to carry so you can use the courses of treatments recommended herein.

For help in a hurry, find the pages covering treatment of your problem by referring first to the Problem Treatment-Finder pages at the front of the book. In general, related problems that require the same pattern of treatment are grouped by individual chapter.

But, please always remember—there's no substitute for using good judgment!

# 2

---

## CUTS IN THE WILDERNESS

THE MOST COMMON OUTDOOR INJURIES are cuts, followed by sprains and strains, bruises, and then fractures. Hands and fingers are hurt most often, then feet and toes, and next, legs. One out of every four injuries coming to the attention of the U. S. Forest Service is caused by hand tools, such as axes and knives.

• *Tetanus*

Everybody, city and backwoods people alike, should be immunized against tetanus *before* the injury rather than after. If an individual has not had such immunization, then, at the time of the injury, tetanus antitoxin must be administered. There are certain risks in the use of this latter and it is impractical to carry it in a first aid kit. It protects for no longer than six weeks. This is called a *passive immunity*.

It is much better to be actively immunized. This may require only one tetanus injection, since most people already have been immunized in their past. At the most, it should require no more than two injections.

Upon showering one night, a man who that day had cut his lawn with a rotary power mower noticed a drop of blood low on his leg. Apparently a small rock had been picked up by the mower and had nicked him. He thought nothing of it at the time. Three weeks later, he ached when he got up and noticed that he had trouble opening his jaw to drink orange juice. That night he was in the hospital, and only heroic efforts saved him. This points out that of itself the severity of the injury is not a sure guide as to the need for tetanus immunization.

● *Treatment of Cuts*

The object of treatment of lacerations is the stopping of bleeding, apposition of the skin edges to promote healing with a minimum of scarring, and prevention of infection.

If the bleeding is heavy, this will have to be stopped first. It is surprising how bleeding usually will stop spontaneously, even in the nastiest cuts. The bleeding, even in a completely severed finger, usually will stop with only pressure over the bleeding area.

## • Using a Compress

The first thing to do, then, is to make *steady,* firm pressure over the cut with a folded gauze, handkerchief, or whatever is available. Do not keep dabbing, as many do, and do not keep looking to see what is going on beneath the compress. Hold the compress for a minimum of five minutes before looking. The chances are that this will have stopped, or at least controlled, all or most of the bleeding.

## • Tourniquets

If there still is active bleeding, the process should be repeated. Only if the bleeding is uncontrollable should one resort to a tourniquet. In routine practice, a doctor might need to use one only about once in fifteen years. A little blood, to be sure, is frightening to most people, but blood loss almost always is overestimated by the inexperienced. Get a quarter of a cup of blood about a room and many persons would estimate that a quart or more has been lost.

If most people would just do what has been outlined above and keep calm, it would end the matter. Most major arteries are well protected, but if an artery is severed, it will squirt blood* at each contraction of the heart, and when pressure will not

---

* As distinguished from the otherwise slow seepage of blood associated with cut or torn veins, many of which are very small.

slow the bleeding a tourniquet should be applied. This can be improvised from a rolled handkerchief, tied loosely between the wound and the heart and *as close to the wound as possible,* then tightened with a twisted stick. It should be just tight enough to control the bleeding while other preparations are carried out. Loosen it each eight to ten minutes. Naturally, this applies to the extremities.

There are no arteries on the face or body that need tourniquets. All arteries spurt, but only the big ones of the extremities might require such drastic treatment. The large vessels of the neck are deep, and pressure will control them also.

With the bleeding now controlled, we can proceed to the next step. (If it is not controlled, we will have to use a special clamp called a *hemostat.* The use of this will be described later in this chapter under the heading, Using the Mosquito Hemostat.)

• *Cleaning the Wound*

The wound should be cleaned next. If it is a clean knife or axe cut, irrigation with drinking water may be adequate. If the wound is dirty and contaminated with foreign material, all bits of dirt, twigs, and the like should be meticulously picked out with the tips of the hemostat. Then the wound should be gently but thoroughly irrigated with soapy water until clean. Do the job well. There is no hurry.

There is no place for the use of alcohol, Merthiolate, or similar antiseptics in these injuries, although year after year first aid books tell you to douse wounds liberally with them. It is true that these substances kill germs, but they also kill tissue, and using them in open wounds will devitalize (kill) tissue. Because germs grow best in devitalized tissue, and some germs are always present, you can see that these preparations set the stage for a future wound infection. At the very least, they delay rather than hasten healing.

Bits of frayed and devitalized tissue are best trimmed off with manicure scissors. This usually is painless because the tissue already is torn loose and is without feeling. Frequently some small amount of bleeding restarts during the cleansing, and again this will respond to pressure. In dirty wounds, it is best to use water which has been boiled for five minutes at sea level, and an additional minute for each extra 1,000 feet of altitude, then cooled.

The best way to handle a cut or scrape is to wash it well with plenty of soap and water, dry it well, and apply a dressing. If the wound is oozy and you feel the dressing might stick to it, a plastic-like absorbent tissue called Telfa should be put over the wound first and then covered with a gauze flat. Telfa can be bought in different sizes in sterile packages in any drug store. No dressing will ever stick when it is used. Never use an ointment on a wound unless it is already infected.

## • Butterfly Tape for Gaping Cuts

If the wound is gaping, it will have to be brought together. This is done most easily with a Butterfly. A Butterfly is a plastic tape which, as illustrated, is applied across the laceration to pull and hold the edges together. This will suffice in most cases. For deep cuts in fingers and other places subject to much movement, however, a stitch may be better.

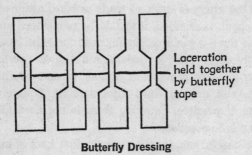

Laceration held together by butterfly tape

**Butterfly Dressing**

## • Using the Mosquito Hemostat

The hemostat doubles both as a needle-holder in the necessity of suture and as a means of stopping arterial bleeding. Hemostats come in many sizes. The small size is called a Mosquito. It is, in essence, a self-locking, needle-nose plier. It also is useful in extracting slivers (especially from beneath a fingernail), fishhooks, thorns, and so on. It also can be used for repair jobs. On one occasion the spring of my spinning reel bail came out of its socket during a fishing trip. The small Mosquito clamp was the only way to hold it and slip it back into its recess. Any surgical supply store has these, and the price is about four dollars.

The Mosquito is used to stop bleeding by grasping the end of the bleeding artery, with as little tissue as possible, and clamping it. It will lock automatically. This crushes the end of the artery, and if left on five minutes, this often is enough.

If the artery is large, or starts to bleed again when the clamp is released, it should be re-clamped and a tie of three-0 plain catgut taken around the base of the bleeder. This is tied with a simple overhand knot, the clamp released, and a second overhand knot, and even a third knot secured. Square the knots, if possible. Squaring them is not hard to do with a little practice.

Be careful not to pull after the first knot is made and the clamp is released, *or the ligature will pull off.** It helps if someone can hold the handle down so the tip of the hemostat shows when the first ligature loop is taken.

This is not a painful operation, normally, and novocaine will not have to be used at this point. It is surprising how insensitive the tissues are beneath skin level. Now, remove the clamp and make second and third knots. Again, do not pull on the knots as

---

* Were one to practice on a piece of meat at home, it would soon come easily.

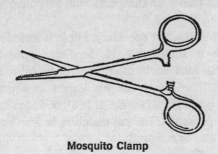

**Mosquito Clamp**

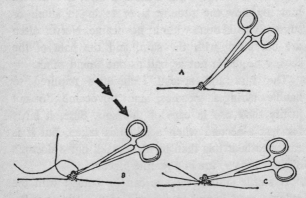

**Use of Hemostat to Clamp a Bleeder**

A. Small bite of bleeder taken in clamp. B. Swing clamp down. This allows ligature to be looped around clamp and allows tip of clamp to show to allow ligature to pass under it. C. Complete overhand knot. Remove clamp and lay down second knot; do this without tugging or the entire ligature will come off. Practice clamping and putting a line around a piece of wool cloth.

[ 27 ]

they are made, or the knots will be pulled off the tissue.

All this is rarely necessary, but it is included here in case it should be. If there are several large bleeders, each is handled separately in a similar fashion. The catgut can be bought at about sixty cents a package, all sterile. It is a good idea to carry several packages. The gut dissolves in time and does not have to be removed.

● *Suturing*

If an individual is far from a doctor, it behooves him to know the rudiments of taking a stitch or suture. This is done without novocaine. Nerves often are cut along with the skin, and the pain of the sewing needle is not as bad as one would think.

The fuss and special techniques required to handle syringes, needles, and novocaine do not justify their use in care of this sort. Sure, it hurts for just a second when a stitch is taken, but it is easier to bear this than to try to seek out a doctor's office when you are in a remote place.

A sterile suture package can be bought with the nylon thread joined to the end of a cutting needle. I use size three-0 for everywhere except the face, where I use five-0. Though five-0 is finer and has less tendency to leave a scar, either size is all right elsewhere. The cut is first washed with soap and water, dried, and then sutured. The needle is held with the small Mosquito clamp, as illustrated.

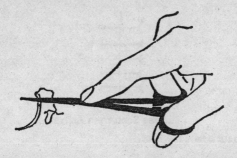

**Method of Holding Needle in Clamp before Suturing**

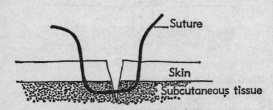

Suture

Skin

Subcutaneous tissue

**Method of Taking a Suture**

Note that stitch is taken just beneath the skin.

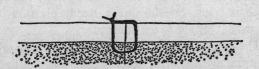

**Tie Nylon to One Side of Cut as Shown**

**Sutures Seen from Above**

Snip here below the knot.

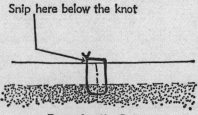

Snip here below the knot

**Removing the Suture**

Pull stitch out by knotted end.

Once the stitch is taken, the suture is tied and cut with the scalpel blade. The ends are left a quarter of an inch long to facilitate removal in seven days. The clamp can substitute as a pair of tweezers to pull out the severed stitch. Any bleeding that occurs from the wound usually stops when the stitch is taken, or with direct, steady pressure over the wound for five to ten minutes.

The suture is taken through the skin. It is taken *only* through the skin, never deeper into the underlying fat or muscle. Anyone who has ever skinned an animal will readily visualize the thickness of skin, which is never more than a quarter of an inch. By not going any deeper, no vital structure will ever be encountered. The only possible source of difficulty might be in hitting a blood vessel. If this happens, simply pull the suture through and out of the skin and take it in another spot a little above or below the one that caused the trouble. The bleeding always will stop with pressure for a minute or so.

One word of caution! Never suture *close to an eyelid*. The healing may pull the skin into a distorted position and cause difficulties later. In general, taking a stitch sounds formidable, but it's really quite simple.

## • *Scalp Lacerations*

These always bleed profusely and invariably stop with pressure alone. Shave the hair from the edge of the laceration. Butterflies rarely work here as there is too much tendency to pull apart. Take one or two sutures where needed, using a three-0 nylon suture. A stitch in the scalp always bleeds at the entrance and exit of the needle. Ignore it. It will stop.

## • *Facial Lacerations*

These are more difficult because the face is more sensitive, because it is desirable to avoid scarring, and because the face has a rich blood supply and bleeds profusely. Cuts here heal faster, and usually with less infections, because of this increased blood supply. Use five-0 suture here to minimize stitch marks, and remove the sutures in four days instead of the customary week.

● *Lip Lacerations*

Suture any lip lacerations as above. If the cut extends through to the mouth, suture only the outside, never the inside, which is left alone.

● *Mouth and Tongue*

The mouth and tongue rarely need sutures. They heal well by themselves. It is better to leave them alone.

● *Lacerations of Fingers*

Suturing is little problem, but be on the watch for loss of finger function due to cut tendons. If a tendon is cut and one or more of the fingers will not work, splint the affected finger or fingers and seek medical help. There is no hurry. A doctor probably would postpone a tendon repair for at least three weeks.

● *Loss of Tip of Finger*

The loss of the tip of a finger by saw or axe is a

nasty problem. The wound cannot be sutured without special skill. If no doctor is available, it will be best to leave it open and allow it to "granulate in," although this may take weeks. It will have to be covered during this period, preferably with an antibiotic ointment and Telfa gauze to prevent sticking.

## • Chest, Abdomen, and Back Lacerations

Lacerations of the chest, abdomen, and back present no problem unless they are deep and enter the chest or abdominal cavity. In this event the patient should be put on an antibiotic and at rest, and expert help should be sought as soon as possible. As described elsewhere, if air is sucked in and out through a chest wound with breathing, use a vaseline-covered patch to plug the hole.

Superficial wounds of the abdomen may sometimes be deeper than they look. When doubt exists as to the depth, the injured should be evacuated at once, before the signs of peritonitis* appear. However, before one panics and gets the Air Rescue Service to risk its men and equipment, let him at least reflect how the wound was made. This will give him some idea of how deep it may be. A slight barbwire scratch of the abdomen obviously isn't going to penetrate into the inner cavity and cause peritonitis. A fall on a sharp stick or a bullet wound may. Some judgment must be used before deciding what to do.

---

* Peritonitis—Acute inflammation of the abdomen's lining membrane.

● *Old Lacerations—Care*

Lacerations fourteen or more hours old should be left alone. Bring them roughly together with butterflies and allow them to heal from the bottom up. This may take several weeks or longer.

The above also applies to very bruised, irregular, and dirty lacerations, which almost always become infected. Gunshot wounds are a good example. So are crushing blows that tear the skin open.

● *Gunshot Wounds*

Naturally, these vary in severity according to the structure or structures involved, and range from minor to fatal. Those of the head, chest, and abdomen need expert attention.

Any bullet wound in the abdomen can be assumed to have perforated an intestine or artery until proven otherwise. The person should eat or drink nothing, and must be gotten to a medical facility. Do not waste time bringing the doctor to the patient.

A chest bullet wound may or may not heal without help. Play it safe, since most are serious. Cover the wound and evacuate the patient. Sometimes one encounters a sucking type of chest wound where the air sucks in and out with each breath. This upsets the whole heart and lung system, and the hole must be sealed shut. Applying one-half inch thicknesses of large gauze flats, well-buttered with vaseline (margarine or any other greasy substance will do in an emergency), and sealing the whole thing well with tape, will close the air leak.

Wounds of the extremities usually are not critical unless a major artery is involved. (See Suturing.) The wound should be irrigated with sterile water. Sterilize water, boil it five minutes at sea level and an extra minute for each additional 1,000 feet of elevation, then cool it. From healthy tissue, which has a normal appearance and bleeds when cut into, frayed and loose tissue must be trimmed off with manicure or other scissors.

Do not suture gunshot wounds. Infection and tetanus are always a problem here because these are dirty, penetrating injuries. Start an antibiotic. Tetanus immunization should be up-to-date. Do not probe for bullets. This is a job for the X-ray and skilled hands. Seek help, even if it cuts a trip short. If a bone is suspected of having been broken, apply a splint.

# 3

## SPRAINS IN THE BACK COUNTRY

THE BIGGEST PROBLEM here is the differentiation between a sprain and a fracture. Naturally, a positive diagnosis will have to depend on the X-ray. In the woods you will have to do the best you can. Some general guidelines may help.

● *Sprain or Fracture*

First, a sprain is the result of stress and strain on the supporting ligaments of a joint. This almost always occurs as a result of force. If the force is severe enough, some of the ligaments may be pulled loose from their attachments. A sprain causes swelling; there is pain with motion of the affected part.

If ligaments have been pulled, the part must be put at rest to allow the ligaments to re-attach and to strengthen themselves. One would hardly expect the roots of a bush to re-attach themselves if they were pulled loose each day. The body is no different. A badly sprained wrist or ankle should be put to rest for seven to fourteen days, or even longer if symptoms persist.

The main problem in handling sprains and fractures in the wilderness is that without X-ray facilities one can never be sure what he is dealing with. Orthopedic procedures, at best, take three to eight weeks under ideal circumstances. It takes the courage of conviction, which the individual may lose as time goes by, to treat something for weeks without certain knowledge respecting just what he's treating. Nevertheless, here are some guidelines which may help simplify a complicated subject.

• *Wrist and Ankle*

Generally, as to whether it's sprain or fracture, the hardest areas to decide on are the wrist and the ankle. A fracture or sprain can cause swelling and pain with motion which may persist for weeks. If an ankle or a wrist is badly swollen, apply an elastic Ace bandage, leave it in place for a month, and use the part gingerly.

Naturally, this assumes that there is no evident gross deformity of the bone that would make you suspect a fracture. The worst that could be present then is a simple, non-displaced fracture of the ends of the leg or arm bones, and non-use for a month would probably let you squeak by. Under ideal circumstances a cast would be applied from the toes to the knee, or from the hand to the elbow in the case of a wrist fracture, and kept on for six weeks.

● *Back Sprains*

Any back injury not resulting from a blow can be assumed to be a sprain. It can be assumed that there is nothing out of place. In eighteen years of medical practice, I have seen countless bad backs, but have yet to see one out of place.

Rest for two to seven days in flexion* (pillow under knees and back, as shown in the drawing) results in healing the back ligaments. In minor cases, rest and aspirin suffice. The associated pain is caused by

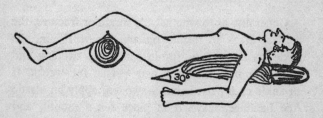

**Back Sprain**

A pillow under knees and under upper back flexes the back on the pelvis and takes the pull off the back muscles.

---

* Flexion—the bending or curving of a limb toward the body.

muscle spasm; putting the muscles to rest permits healing.

● *Shoulder, Elbow, and Knee Sprains*

Shoulder sprains and elbow sprains may require that the affected part be put at rest in a sling. Knee sprains can be rested in an elastic bandage. See the illustration.

**Use of Sling—Shoulder or Arm Sprains**

Note that part from under arm goes straight up to the neck on the same side as the side of the injured arm.

● *Finger Sprains*

Finger joint sprains are best put in an aluminum or plastic finger splint, as shown in the accompanying drawings. It is not a bad idea to carry two or three of these splints. They are light. A few circular loops of tape easily secure them.

● *Neck Sprains*

Do not use heat for neck sprains, although heat does help other sprains. Take aspirin by the clock,

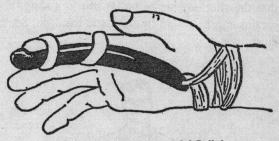

**Finger in Long Commercial Splint**

These can be made from any available material. Useful in sprains or fractures of fingers.

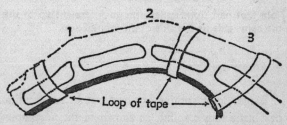

**Short Commercial Splint Taped to Sprained Finger**

A short or long splint can be used to splint bone on either side of joint. Thus, short splint for Joint 1 or 2, long splint for Joint 3.

two each four hours. Neck sprains are slow to mend. If full motion is possible, even though painful, it is unlikely that a fracture or dislocation is present.

● *When to Use Hot and Cold Compresses*

Apply cold compresses for the first twelve to eighteen hours to reduce and prevent swelling. After that generally use heat to lessen the swelling.

## 4

# FROM THE WAIST UP—
# FRACTURES AND DISLOCATIONS

THESE COMMON ORTHOPEDIC PROBLEMS can be difficult. The methods next described will not always work. Even under ideal conditions, it may be impossible to reduce a bone, or to hold a bone in place once it is reduced. This also applies to dislocations. Soft tissue may interpose between the parts, making a permanent reduction impossible.

Fractures should be handled by doctors whenever possible. Some general principles nevertheless will assist those away from the doctor to understand how such accidents should be handled and what to expect.

• *Shoulder Dislocations*

The head of the arm bone is obviously out of place. Comparison of both shoulders is helpful in deciding. The head of the arm bone can be displaced forward or backward.

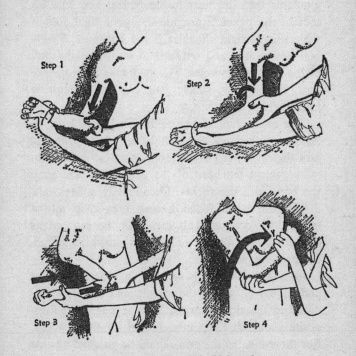

### Reduction of Shoulder Dislocation

A 4-step alternative method to the "Foot-in-Armpit" method. Step 1. Downward traction. Step 2. Now, while pulling down, swing the forearm outward to externally rotate the dislocated arm bone, all the time maintaining the downward traction. Keep the elbow out from the body all the time. Step 3. Now force the elbow across the chest. Step 4. Last step. In one smooth motion, swing the wrist without hesitation across to the shoulder on the opposite side. This will snap the shoulder into place.

[ 43 ]

First, try to reduce the dislocation by having the patient lie down. With a stockinged foot, the manipulator then lies next to the patient and puts his foot in the patient's armpit. Use your right foot if the patient's right shoulder is the one hurt. Slowly pull downwards and outward to overcome the pull of the shoulder muscles. This may take several minutes. Use a slow, steady pull. Do not attempt to jerk anything into place.

The edge of the foot can be used as a lever to lift or pry against the arm bone. Now bring the arm slightly inward as the foot, acting like a fulcrum, pries against the head of the bone. This will snap the bone into the socket. Occasionally a backward dislocation, when reduced, may then snap into a forward dislocation. This can again be reduced as described, or it can be reduced as shown in the accompanying pictures.

After the shoulder is reduced, a generous cotton pad should be put in the armpit, and the arm bandaged to the side, with the hand resting on the opposite shoulder. Keep immobilized for three weeks. For three months the arm should be guarded against further injury; no wood chopping, paddling, etc. Failure to do this may cause another dislocation, or chronic recurrent dislocations may then ensue.

• *Fracture of the Collar Bone*

This usually occurs from a direct blow or a fall. There is an obvious deformity of the clavicle (collar

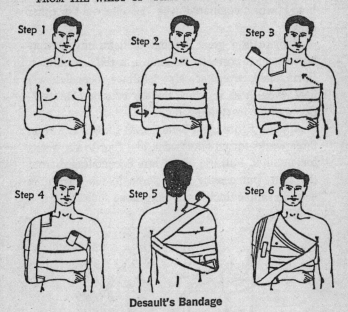

**Desault's Bandage**

For holding arm in place in shoulder dislocation.

Step 1. A pad is put in each armpit. Step 2. The pads are held in place with several turns about the chest of bandage. Step 3. Pass the bandage around the back and up toward the injured side. Note pad on collar bone. Step 4. The bandage goes over the injured shoulder and down to elbow. The bandage passes over the elbow and back across the back to the good armpit. Step 5. View of same from back. Step 6. The bandage then passes up to the injured shoulder again, over it this time, and down the back of the injured arm, then around to the front of the injured arm and obliquely across chest to complete the Figure 8 type loop. Make several of these Figure 8s with the finished result as shown in Step 6. If necessary, this can be modified to place the hand onto the chest with the loops going over the hand to hold it flat against the chest. This would be good to hold a broken forearm against the chest.

[ 45 ]

bone) when compared with the one on the other side.

If there is a great amount of deformity, it may be somewhat corrected as shown in the illustrations. Fortunately, even grossly deformed clavicles will heal, even those in which there is considerable over-riding of the fractured ends.

Apply a figure eight bandage, as shown. Leave on three weeks for an adolescent, and four to six weeks for an adult. Full use of the arm is encouraged from the start, but a sling from seven to ten days may help. In simple fractures, a sling alone suffices.

**How to Improve the Position of a Clavicle Fracture**

A folded towel between the shoulder blades will increase the leverage if necessary. See text.

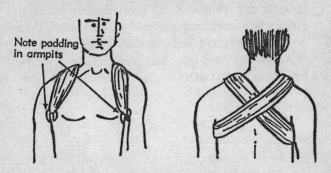

**Figure 8 Bandage Front and Back Views**

Apply with enough tension to pull shoulders somewhat backward much as the straps on a knapsack would work. Apply Ace bandage here and elsewhere under half-stretch or tension. Hold shoulders back while elastic bandage is applied.

● *Back Injuries*

If a fracture is suspected, the patient must be handled properly to prevent injury to the spinal cord. See the illustration. If the individual is able to bend over to touch his toes, and the spine bends in a smooth curve, it is unlikely that any of the vertebrae are fractured. Fractures of the tips of the spinous processes and of the lateral wings that come off the vertebral bodies ordinarily need no treatment.

● *Fracture of the Arm*

Fractures below the upper third of the arm and above the elbow need not be held in accurate apposition with plaster casts. The weight of the arm usually will overcome the pull of the muscles, to set the fracture and keep the ends in apposition.

A hanging arm-type cast arrangement is used, but in the back country a weighted mold made from

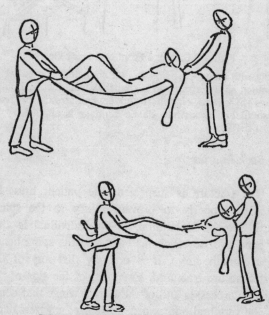

**DON'T DO THIS in Back Injury Cases!**

These are the **wrong ways** of moving patients with back injuries. Instead:   (A.) Transport the patient **face down** on a blanket lifted by **four people,** unless a stretcher is available, or (B.) on a stretcher with a pillow or folded blanket under his waist.

bark, metal, or cardboard—then well padded and weighted—will suffice. Three or four sections of newspaper, with sixteen to twenty pages per section, also make good splints. Eight to ten pounds of weight will do.

⌐Loop sling over wrist taped to splint
⌐ Right-angle splint improvised from bark,
   metal, etc., placed over well-padded arm

**Hanging Arm Cast**

Used to reduce upper arm fractures. Tape enough weight along bottom of cast to make 6 to 8 pounds. Improvise!

Healing takes six to eight weeks, usually. Again, there is no way of accurately timing the healing process, and the decision when healing is enough advanced to allow removing the apparatus usually is made with the benefit of an X-ray. All figures on relative healing periods are estimates for cases under the best of conditions, with no complications.

[ 49 ]

● *Complications—Shoulder Girdle and Upper Arm*

There is enough elasticity in the major blood vessels so that hemorrhage is rarely a problem unless the fracture is compound. A compound fracture is when the bone tears through the flesh and skin to the outside.

The greatest problem is that the important nerves in the armpit become stretched or torn, and the forearm or hand does not function properly or has areas of numbness. The arm should be kept in a sling and at rest; further treatment is a job for the specially trained.

● *Elbow Fractures*

These are nasty, at best. The results often are bad. Put the arm in a sling and seek help. As long as the color and the circulation of the hand remain good, time is not of the essence. In general, no harm is done if several days to a week pass before a fracture anywhere in the body comes under skilled management, providing the area is suitably splinted.

● *Elbow Dislocation*

Reduction is accomplished as shown in the drawings. Pull downward as indicated in Steps 1 and 2. If this does not work, extend the arm as shown in

Step 3 and exert pressure as shown by the arrows. Then flex and proceed as shown in Steps 1 and 2.

After reduction, the arm should be kept as shown

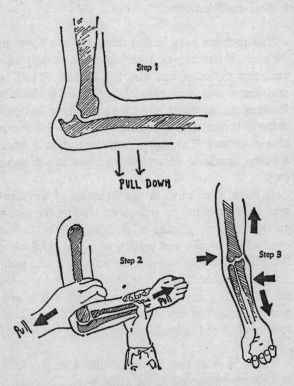

**Handling Elbow Dislocations**

Step 1. Before traction.   Step 2. Then the dislocation snaps back.   Step 3. (Use **only** if Steps 1 and 2 do not work.) Pull down on arm and exert pressure in direction of arrows, then flex to right angle and proceed as in Steps 1 and 2.

in the illustration (Step 1 only, *not* Step 2) for two or three weeks. Motion of the hand and the shoulder should be started immediately, however.

● *Forearm Fractures*

The problem here is that there are two bones in the arm. If one breaks, then one must strongly suspect that the other one also has broken. It can be envisioned that two parallel sticks, each securely fastened to the other at each end, cannot be individually broken and shortened unless the other one also gives way. The only exception to this is when a sharp, localized, direct blow occurs to one bone only.

If there is an obvious misalignment of the forearm bones, attempt to reduce by holding the elbow at right angles, placing a stockinged foot in the bend of the elbow, and pulling with one hand while the other hand tries to mold the ends back into position. Remember that a long, slow pull is best. Do not jerk. Also, any doctor is happy with a fifty percent apposition of the bone ends. They do not have to be end to end in perfect apposition to get a good result.

The arm must then be immobilized so the wrist and elbow do not move for eight weeks. Normally, this is done with a plaster cast, but an alternative arrangement is shown which may suffice. Even in the best of circumstances these fractures may not hold in position. You can't do more than try.

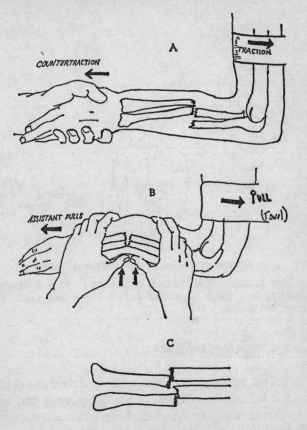

## Handling Forearm Fractures

A. Fracture before reduction.   B. Alternate method of reducing forearm fracture. Towel secured above elbow supplies countertraction to assistant's pull. Fingers mold fractured ends into position.   C. A 50% apposition of bone ends (half of each bone touching). This is an acceptable result, and bones will heal well if left in this position without moving.

[ 53 ]

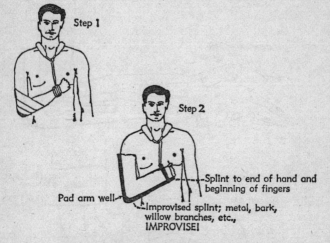

Step 1

Step 2

Splint to end of hand and beginning of fingers

Pad arm well

Improvised splint; metal, bark, willow branches, etc., IMPROVISE!

**Method of Holding Forearm Without Plaster**

Step 1. (Also used in elbow dislocation.)   Step 2. Now add padding and splint to further secure elbow and wrist. Wrist must not move!

- *Fractures of the Wrist*

This usually occurs from a fall on the outstretched hand. There is pain, loss of use of the wrist, and an upward displacement of the hand which often looks forklike.

To reduce, grasp the hand as in shaking hands, break up any impaction* as shown, and reduce by pulling upwards, then outwards and downwards, as indicated. The forearm from the palm to the elbow

---

* Impaction—lodgment of something.

must then be splinted for six weeks. Encourage use of the fingers from the start.

● *Finger Fractures*

Identification of the fracture and the degree of displacement is easier here because the bones can

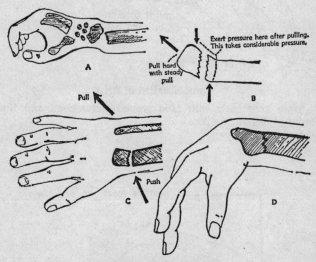

**Treating the Wrist Fracture**

A. Note upward displacement of wrist giving the wrist a cocked-up position. Note how weak the grip is in this position. The downward position of the hand must be restored.   B. To reduce, first pull hand up and away from forearm, and exert pressure on end fragment.   C. Now pull down and out toward small finger.   D. Last, pull hand into flexed position to complete set.

easily be felt. Reduction is simpler because the muscle pull on the bone ends is easier to overcome.

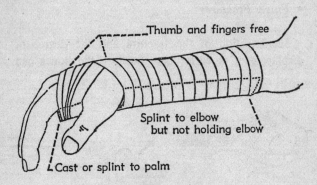

Thumb and fingers free

Splint to elbow
but not holding elbow

Cast or splint to palm

**Immobilization of Wrist**

Wrap generously with tape around and around arm from bases of fingers to elbow.

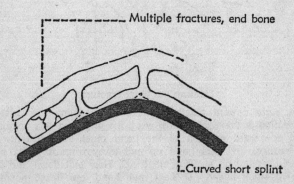

Multiple fractures, end bone

Curved short splint

**Handling Fractured End Bones**

## • End Bones

Fractures here are usually crushing, or they are multiple fractures. Displacement (parts out of place) is rare. Protect the end of the finger for fourteen days with a short splint to include the joint and a portion of the bone above it.

## • Middle Bone Fracture

A middle bone fracture of the finger may bend up or down, depending on where the break occurs. It is determined by the pull of the muscle tendon attachments. The illustrations show how these should be held. Three weeks usually suffice.

## • Fracture Close to Knuckles

A fracture of the bone closest to the knuckles is usually reduced by traction. Bend into flexion, with the finger clenched. Never splint straight out. Ideally, flex over a roll of gauze, as shown, then tape into position.

## • Nasal Fractures

The nose obviously is pushed to one side. With the fingers on either side of the bridge of the nose, or by grasping the nose between the thumb and fore-

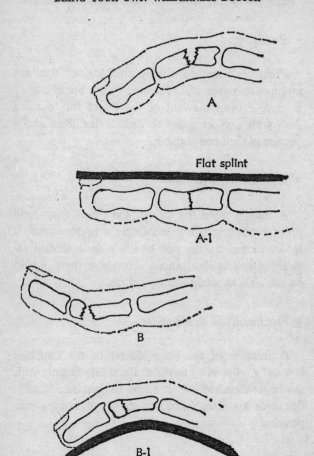

Flat splint

A

A-1

B

B-1

**Finger—Middle Bone Fractures**

A. Downward fracture.   A-1. Flat padded splint to hold up downward fracture.   B. Upward fracture.   B-1. Hold upward fracture over metal splint and tape securely.

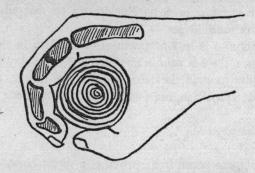

**Fracture of Finger Bone Closest to Knuckles**

Finger and whole hand, if necessary, flexed over roller bandage. Maintain for three weeks.

finger, the nose can actually be pushed back into position without too much difficulty.

Beware of working on the nose that is not fractured. Because of soft tissue swelling beside the nose and beneath the eye, the nose may look deformed. Carefully feeling the nose usually will disclose whether or not the bones are in the midline.

The displaced nose usually snaps back with a pop. Nosebleed that occurs with it is not a serious problem and stops shortly. Cold compresses minimize swelling.

• *Fractures of the Jaw and Face*

With fractures of the face, there is pain, swelling, and deformity. Treatment is best left to skilled hands.

[ 59 ]

There is no emergency. Repair can be delayed a week or much longer.

This also is true of fractures of the jaw. In this instance, there is pain in chewing, and there may be inability to hold the teeth together. A dentist, as well as a physician, can usually treat jaw fractures.

● *Dislocated Jaw*

This can occur from yawning, a direct blow, or attempting to bite an apple, or such. The jaw is held open, and a prominence can be felt on the side where the jaw is dislocated. The dislocation may also occur on both sides.

Reduction is accomplished by wrapping the thumbs well in something like a towel and then inserting them in the mouth. Downward pressure is exerted on the lower rear teeth (molars), while the fingers lift the chin,

The jaw will go back into place with a pop. It is essential that the thumbs be padded to prevent their being cut by the patient's teeth.

● *Rib Fractures*

(See under Chest Problems, chapter 6.)

● *Fractures of Hand Bones*

Fractures of the metacarpal, or long bones of the hand, occur from a blow directed into the knuckles,

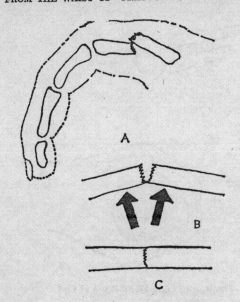

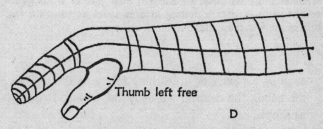

Thumb left free

**Fracture of Long Hand Bone in Middle**

A. Reduce by traction on finger. Attempt to mold ends into place. B. Pull in long axis of finger, then push up as shown. This engages ends. C. Now straighten. D. After straightening, hold in splint from tips of fingers to upper forearm (long splint on affected finger); then splint all and tape.

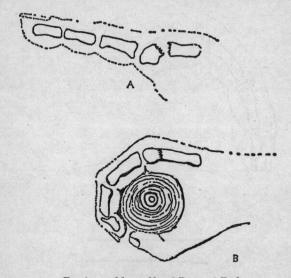

**Fracture of Long Hand Bone at End**

When fracture is at the end of the metacarpal, as shown in A, hand must be taped or secured over pad or roller gauze, as shown in B, before putting in arm splint as used for fracture of bone in the middle.

such as a punch or a crushing injury to the top of the hand. The deformity usually can be felt. Reduce as shown.

In some oblique fractures the pieces will not hold and have to be secured with traction by putting a pin through the bones. This is a job for a doctor. If the metacarpal is broken near the end, it may have to be held in the clenched-fist position.

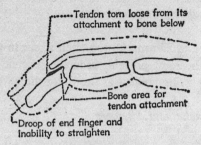

Tendon torn loose from its attachment to bone below

Bone area for tendon attachment

Droop of end finger and inability to straighten

**Trigger Finger**

- *Trigger Finger*

This problem sometimes occurs when the end of a finger is struck. The extensor tendon is torn loose. Immobilize, as shown, with the finger in forced extension. Hold six weeks. Results are often poor.

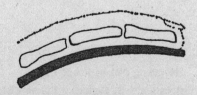

**Splint with Trigger Finger Forced Upward**

● *Dislocation of Thumb*

Reduce as shown. All too often a tear in the capsule of the joint prevents reduction except by surgical means. Immobilize as shown for three weeks.

● *Pain Relief and Aftercare*

Before setting fractures, take two aspirin with codeine tablets or two one-grain Darvon Compound tablets, then wait thirty minutes before manipulation.

Watch all parts carefully after reductions for excess swelling and bluish discoloration. If circulation does not improve after the splint is loosened, remove the splint, even if it means loss of the desired position of fracture. It is better to do this than to lose an extremity.

Use Darvon Compound or codeine to control pain for the next several days, if necessary, and keep the affected area elevated to minimize swelling.

**Handling Dislocation of Thumb**

**A.** Thumb dislocation.   **B.** Reducing thumb dislocation.   **C.** Proper method of splinting and taping with thumb held out.

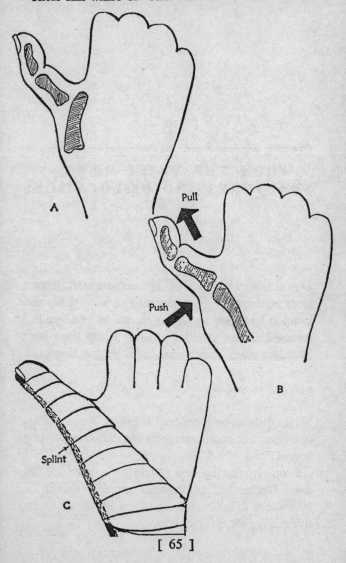

# 5

## FROM THE WAIST DOWN— FRACTURES AND DISLOCATIONS

A FAR NORTH FRIEND of my collaborator, thrown from his horse in the wilderness, once set a hip dislocation by strapping his leg to one tree and pulling on another tree with his arms until the bone went back into place—an extreme measure, but it worked.

• *Hip Dislocation*

Hip dislocation is reduced either by direct traction or by the four maneuvers shown in the accompanying figures.

Properly, the leg then should be splinted for ten days. During healing, crutches should be used for four weeks to relieve the leg of weight. Avoid excessive activity for three months.

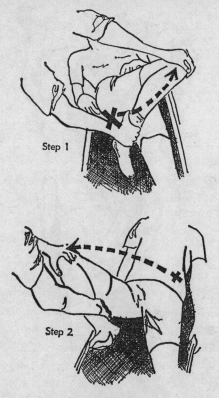

Step 1

Step 2

## Reduction of Hip Dislocation

Step 1. Swing heel and raise up as shown. Step 2. Keep knee bent and ankle in same relative position. Swing out knee (external rotation). Step 3. Steady leg with left hand. Pull ankle down and leg turned out (externally rotated) somewhat more than drawing indicates. Step 4. Complete straightening the leg and finish rotating leg from external rotation (Charlie Chaplin style) with foot out to neutral position and force knee into knock-kneed position. Do in one smooth motion.

[ 67 ]

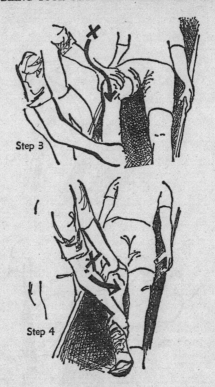

Step 3

Step 4

## • *Location of the Hip*

Most people do not know where their hip is. It is not a back joint, as commonly supposed, and it is not the pelvic crest just below the belt line, as many think. From the point where the inside leg meets the body, the hip joint is located laterally toward the outside of the leg. By placing a hand over this area and moving the leg back and forth you can fix it firmly in mind.

### • Hip Fracture

The leg turns outward, and the leg is shortened. Gently swinging the foot from the turned-out position to the proper position causes pain and is resisted by the patient, but slight movement of a dislocation will not be so painful.

There is nothing the layman can do for hip fracture. Its treatment requires a hospital procedure.

### • Thigh Bone (Femur) Fracture

This is a serious fracture that needs professional attention. It often is accompanied by shock and severe pain. Splint as shown.

---- Pad in armpit

**Thigh Bone Fractures Are Serious**

Splint and prepare patient for transport.

## • Kneecap and Lower Leg Fracture

These likewise are nasty fractures and the results are often bad. Healing is prolonged, often taking months. These injuries are not treatable in the bush.

## • Ankle Fractures

A simple fracture of the lower leg bones just above the ankle has the appearance of a badly sprained ankle. Splint, to hold the foot at right angles to the leg, up to just below the knee. Wrap with elastic bandage to hold in place. Bear no weight on the injured leg for six weeks.

As pointed out, it may be impossible to tell a fracture from a bad sprain, and if the sprain is bad enough, the treatment just prescribed for a fractured ankle should be continued for four to six weeks to allow the ligaments to heal. Squeezing the two leg bones together often causes pain in an ankle fracture, but it is not an infallible sign of a fracture.

## • Heel Bone

Bad and multiple breaks require a doctor. Simple fractures will heal in eight to ten weeks with the foot in a splint, as for ankle fracture, and the use of a crutch.

● *Toes and Long Foot Bones*

Fractures in the toes and the long foot bones, the metatarsals, will heal in eight weeks if no weight is borne on them, and if they are put in a splint as for the ankle. The splint is carried to below the knee. Maintaining accurate position of the hand bone is important to the hand's proper functioning, but in the case of the foot, correct positioning, while desirable, is of lesser importance.

# 6

## CHEST PROBLEMS IN
## THE WOODS

THIS CHAPTER deals with the problems of rib fractures, pulmonary edema, heart attack, pneumothorax, and rapid heart rate.

● *Rib Fractures*

These are not handled like ordinary fractures. The problem is not with the break, but with the underlying lung and the problems that go with improper treatment.

Squeezing the ribs together from front to back, with one hand over the vertebrae and the other over the breastbone, produces pain over the broken rib area.

Rib fractures need no treatment in themselves. They need not be splinted, and they invariably will heal. The rib is the only bone that will regenerate—a whole section of rib can be removed surgically and it will grow back.

The important thing with rib fractures is *to do nothing*. Let's explain. Rib fractures hurt. They hurt every minute of the day. They hurt when you get out of bed. They hurt with every breath. They hurt when one gets back into bed. But they heal in three to five weeks. Try to tape them to prevent the pain and surely a pleurisy or pneumonia will result.

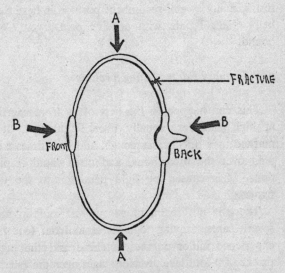

**Rib Fractures**

Compressing the chest by squeezing at points A—A or B—B will cause the rib cage to bow painfully at the fracture site.

The lungs must keep expanding to work. If this is prevented by taping, trouble will ensue. The ticket is to control the pain with aspirin and codeine, or Darvon Compound. The ribs and lungs then will take care of themselves without complications.

Once in a while the rib cage actually is caved in from a severe injury. The sharp fragments of the rib may actually tear the lung. There may be blueness of the fingernails or the lips, and there is marked shortness of breath. There may be blood in the sputum. This is a serious matter and needs expert medical attention. Put the patient at absolute bed rest. Usually a semi-recumbent position is best. Seek help. Control pain with codeine or Darvon Compound.

### • Pulmonary Edema (Lung Swelling)

This can happen to the best of us from exertion at high altitudes, usually over 9,000 feet. It is marked by a dry, brassy cough, and sometimes chest pain over the breastbone, and often rapid respirations. It is caused by fluid passing into the lung tissues.

There is no treatment except rest and, in more severe cases, moving to a lower altitude. One may experience minor degrees of this from climbing at the 12,000-foot level. Minor stages, as manifested by a tickling cough, can be ignored. Naturally, you should refrain from smoking. It subsides in one to three days.

## • *Heart Attack*

Everyone knows that this is a serious problem, one that needs help and expert attention. Whole books have been written about this, and the subject can be exceedingly technical. The main thing is to recognize the classical attack.

Under the best of circumstances, it may be difficult to diagnose a borderline case. The classical example is dramatic, however, and worth describing. Usually during exertion, rarely while at rest, there is a severe frontal chest pain over the heart and breastbone area. It is may radiate up into the left neck or down the inner side of the left arm.

The patient ceases what he is doing—stops in his tracks—he just doesn't finish what he is doing. Often he has a sense of impending disaster. The skin becomes pale and sweaty. The pulse becomes rapid.

There is little that can be done for him in the back country except to have him avoid all activity. Absolute bed rest is necessary. The important thing is to recognize the problem and seek help.

## • *Pneumothorax*

This can happen to those in the best of health. As a matter of fact, it is common among those who are young and in the prime of physical condition.

A small bleb (a blister or bubble) on the lung

ruptures, and air leaks between the lung and the chest wall where it does not belong. There is one-sided chest pain, shallow respiration, and shortness of breath. Careful observation of the patient may show a difference in the way the lungs expand, with the affected side moving less than the normal side with each breath.

Again, this needs outside help. The thing to do is to recognize it, identify the problem.

### • Rapid Heart Rate

This is another problem that occurs in normal, healthy people with sound hearts. The pacemaker of the heart simply goes haywire, and the pulse speeds from 160 to 200 beats a minute. The individual feels fatigued, and his pulse or heart rate is rapid.

Standard treatments include holding the breath. Or, induce vomiting by putting a finger in the throat.

Attacks of this type often can also be terminated by drinking three or four ounces of ice-cold water, or by pressing over both eyeballs, with the lids closed, to the point of being downright uncomfortable. This is continued twenty to thirty seconds.

A prime candidate for the problem is the sportsman who works like blazes and ends his week in a lather, anticipating an early start for his trip, then drives 300 miles, eats a hasty supper in a roadside cafe, then belts down a few fast ones at perhaps an altitude to which he has not yet become acclimated.

# 7

---

## SKIN INFECTIONS

THIS CHAPTER deals with various skin problems such as cellulitis, boils, abscesses, intertrigo, contact dermatitis, poison ivy, oak and sumac, hives, and discusses tularemia.

## • Infections (Cellulitis)

This is an infection of the skin from any break of the skin surface. It can follow a puncture wound, an abrasion, or a cut. All people are familiar with its appearance, hence a description is unnecessary.

If the area is open, as with a burn or an abrasion, then an antibiotic ointment is of some help. It serves absolutely no purpose to smear a closed infection, such as a boil or a skin abscess, with ointments, drawing salves, and the like. In general, warm, moist compresses, applied for fifteen to twenty minutes four to six times daily, help localize the infection. Using a saturated solution either of salt or Epsom salts is even better. This is made by stirring the crystals into a cup of water until no more will dissolve. In general, antibiotics are unnecessary.

A more serious problem occurs when red streaks develop from the infected area. This condition may be accompanied by chills or fever. Place the part at complete rest, with a sling in the case of the hand, or bed rest or a crutch, in the case of the legs.

Start an oral antibiotic for three to four days, and treat the affected area with hot, moist compresses, as described above; the more they are used, the better. Under ideal circumstances, they should be used continuously. Usually the streaking will be gone in twenty-four hours.

Often the glands ("kernels") in the armpit or the groin become swollen following an infection of the particular extremity. An antibiotic should be continued until the swelling and the discomfort subside.

• *Boils and Other Abscesses*

These usually come to a head, or the top surface softens. They are best opened when this occurs. It can be hastened with wet heat, as described.

Do not attempt to squeeze an abscess. Nature surrounds the abscess with a protective wall of white blood cells. Squeezing the boil breaks down this protective wall, and the germs are then forced into the adjacent tissues. The infection then is no longer localized, but becomes a more serious diffused one. Open the boil with a single stab incision with the #11 Bard-Parker blade, as illustrated.

----Stab made with #11 blade
----Liquifying debris and pus in abscess
----Surface of skin
----Protective wall of white blood cells
----Zone of inflammatory tissue around abscess

**Cross-Section of Typical Abscess**

● *Danger Area—Face*

There is a danger area on the face that deserves special mention. This area encompasses the upper lip, the nose, and the face immediately adjacent to the nose and beneath the eyes. Any infection in this region drains directly into the brain area without the protection of regional lymph glands ("kernels"). View all infection in this area as potentially serious and treat to the maximum. Above all, *never* squeeze an abscess in this area.

● *Intertrigo (Form of Rash)*

This is a rash and occurs in warm, moist areas of the groin, the armpits, and other skin folds. Keeping the area dry and powdered with talc is the best prevention and treatment. Incidentally, the sometimes used boric acid *is a poison.* One is likely to get in trouble with it. The best thing is not to use it, for its merits are few and its complications many.

● *Contact Dermatitis*

Most typically, this is a weepy, moist area, resulting either from contact with poison oak and the like, or from any other substances to which the individual is allergic or sensitive.

Keep ointments off weepy areas. In general, cool, moist compresses are helpful. Witch hazel is ideal if it is available. Calamine lotion is the old standby, but in the bush relief from itching and irritation, as well as a specific therapeutic effect, can be had from starch baths or compresses. For large areas of the body, a starch bath will do miracles for itching, and for soothing the area.

Stir a cup of starch into a quart of boiling water to make a colloidal suspension. This now is used for compresses, or it can be added to a tub of water for soaking large areas.

(See Cortisone, chapter 17.)

● *Burns and Blisters*

(Discussed under respective heads in chapter 12.)

● *Poison Ivy, Oak, and Sumac*

Contact with these plants causes a skin irritation, first apparent as itchy bumps. Small blisters soon develop. The fluid in these is exceedingly irritating, so that scratching tends to spread the rash.

First, learn what these plants look like and avoid them. Be careful of the fumes of these growths when they are burning, as they can cause serious lung congestion. If you do come in contact with poison ivy, oak, or sumac, wash well with soap and water. Remove your clothing, and wash these before you wear them again.

Try at all costs to avoid scratching the affected areas. Pyribenzamine, 50 mg. each four hours, is usually effective in helping the itch. So is aspirin, two five-grain tablets each four hours. A paste of starch and water—or, better yet, starch boiled with a small amount of water to make a thick, gravy-like concoction—can be applied locally to dry the blisters and to allay itching.

For large affected areas, if you have the facilities, make a starch bath by, first, adding a cup of starch such as flour to a quart of boiling water. This is stirred into a container of lukewarm water in which the patient soaks for fifteen to twenty minutes. The treatment is very soothing. An oatmeal bath can also be used, simply by substituting oatmeal for the starch.

When extreme cases do not respond to any of

the above treatments, use the cortisone, one tablet each four hours as described under Cortisone in chapter 17.

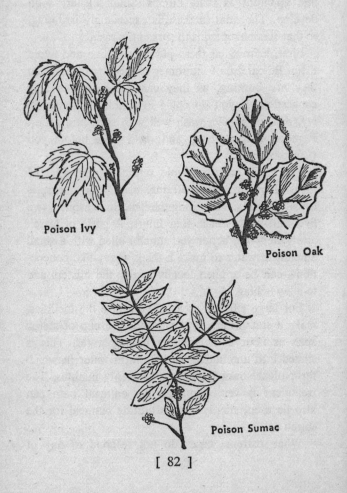

Poison Ivy

Poison Oak

Poison Sumac

● *Hives*

These pesky welts need no description. They itch and are uncomfortable, to say the least. They may be brought on by an insect bite, allergy to some food, or by a combination of factors such as fatigue and uneasy emotions. Treatment by use of laxatives and purgatives is not encouraged. Stay on an antihistaminic (Pyribenzamine 50 mg. each four hours four times daily is a good one). The starch baths described above help. Cortisone also helps.

● *Tularemia*

Tularemia is included in this section as the first sign of it may be a skin ulcer, noted a week or two after skinning a diseased rabbit. Actually, tularemia is a rare illness, but you may fall prey to it in the wilderness. The best prevention is to avoid handling animals that appear to be ill or easy to shoot, such as a rabbit that failed to run when flushed. These animals may be diseased with tularemia.

The disease is commonly acquired through a break in the skin through which the germ enters. It causes an ulcer at the site of entry, followed by enlargement of the regional glands—in the armpit in the case of a hand infection. This, in turn, is followed by systemic symptoms such as fever and a general feeling of being ill, or possibly by pneumonia or by intestinal symptoms resembling typhoid.

Tularemia also may be transmitted by the bite of the deer fly, or of a tick, and in rare instances from bad water, usually contaminated by the urine of a beaver or other rodent.

There is an antibiotic of choice, but Tetracycline or Erythrocin seems to prevent the germ from growing if used for ten days. The drug of choice here is Streptomycin, but this is a tricky drug to use, and since the illness is so rare it is suggested that the individual on his own use the Erythrocin or Tetracycline drug if tularemia is suspected. Incubation period of the illness is seven to fourteen days, plus or minus.

# 8

## STOMACH AND RELATED PROBLEMS

MANY AN OUTDOOR TRIP has been ruined because of nausea, vomiting, diarrhea, or all combined. To a large extent, these are all preventable by using good judgment and suitable precautions. There is a large group of viruses and bacteria responsible for these problems which are acquired through the media of food, flies, water, contaminated hands, or stools.

● *Preventing Stomach Problems*

Prevention includes treating all unknown water chemically, as considered in a moment, or by boiling it for five minutes at sea level, adding one extra minute for each additional 1,000 feet of elevation.

It entails good refrigeration of food, when possible, and the proper care of the food in any event. A salad with mayonnaise cannot be used, left out on a table for an hour or so, and then put back into the camp ice chest. Fish should be promptly cleaned, dried, and put into something such as cheesecloth or ferns, not shoved into a plastic bag that is in and out of the sun all day, and then tossed on the camp table for an hour or so before cleaning.

Fresh eggs need to be kept cool. Never eat food from a bulging can. Don't throw pot scrapings around the camp. They surely will attract flies. Keep food covered. Flies carry germs. The things some intelligent people do when camping and supposedly practicing camp sanitation are fantastic, and yet a little common sense gives the answers to good camp sanitation.

Also, on this subject, choose your eating places carefully when driving away from home, and eat simple foods. Avoid cream pies, custards, mayonnaise, meats with re-warmed gravies, etc. Stay with beef (chicken spoils easily), simple salads, and fruits for dessert.

### • Simple Chemical Water Purification

One can purchase at most sporting goods and drug stores, for about forty cents, a small two-ounce bottle containing one hundred Halazone tablets. Since their purifying action depends upon the release at the proper time of chlorine gas, these should be fresh, the container tightly closed, and its contents dry.

No water purification by chemical means is as dependable as boiling, but two Halazone tablets ordinarily will make a quart of water safe for human consumption in a half hour. If the water is muddy or particularly questionable, it is good insurance to double at least the amount of Halazone, and preferably the time as well.

Care should be taken with chemical purifiers to disinfect all points of contact with the container, so the water, once sterilized, will not be easily reinfected. If a jar or canteen is being used with Halazone, replace the cover loosely and wait two or three minutes so the tablets can dissolve. Then shake the contents thoroughly, allowing some of the fluid to spill out over the top and the lips of the holder. Tighten the cover, then leave it that way for the desired time before using any of the water.

● *Iodine Water Purification Tablets*

Chlorine-releasing compounds cannot be relied upon in semitropical and tropical areas. Water in these regions should be boiled, or when this is not feasible, treated with Iodine Water Purification Tablets. Containing the active Tetraglycine Hydroperiodide, these have been adopted as standard for the armed services of the United States.

The tablets have been proved effective against all common water-borne bacteria as well as the cysts of

Endamoeba histolytica and the cercariae of schistosomiasis. Manufactured as Globaline by WTS Pharmaceuticals, Division of Wallace and Tiernan, Inc., in Rochester, New York 14623, fifty water purification tablets are packaged in a glass bottle with a wax-seal cap. Any drug store can secure these for you. Added to water, each tablet frees eight milligrams of iodine which acts as a purification factor. One tablet will purify one quart of clear water.

These tablets, too, must be kept dry. The bottle, therefore, should be recapped tightly after being opened. Directions for use are:

(1) add one tablet to a quart of clear water in container with cap, two tablets if not clear,

(2) replace cap loosely and wait five minutes,

(3) shake well, allowing a little water to leak out and disinfect the screw threads before tightening container cap,

(4) wait ten minutes before using for any purpose and if water is very cold, wait twenty minutes.

• *Vomiting*

Do not eat or drink anything until the vomiting stops, although the mouth may be moistened with ice chips or cold water.

After the initial wave of vomiting is over, or if only nausea occurs, take a 5 mg. Compazine tablet each four hours until symptoms are gone. Compazine quiets the intestines, stopping spasm and nausea.

In addition to using Compazine for nausea, take one Probanthine tablet each four hours to quiet cramps and spasm.

Take only liquids or sparse amounts of food for the next day or so. Other causes of vomiting besides food poisoning will be discussed below.

● *Diarrhea*

This is caused by the same spasm that incites vomiting, but at the other end of things. If vomiting and diarrhea occur together treat the vomiting first.

Generally, the Probanthine will work better in lower intestinal cramps. The Compazine is not as effective here. Take two Lomotil tablets each three to four hours until the diarrhea is under control, then one three to four times daily for a day or so until things settle down.

Keep the diet simple. Avoid milk. If cramping is excessive, a warm compress placed on the abdomen helps.

Paregoric is excellent for the treatment of a diarrhea, but it is sometimes difficult to carry because it is a liquid. If weight and spillage were no problem one might well carry paregoric in a kit, mixed with milk of bismuth in equal parts. The dosage of paregoric and bismuth is two teaspoons each four hours if diarrhea is not severe; otherwise, two teaspoons after each loose stool until stools slow down, then each two to four hours to control.

If the intestinal disorder is accompanied by fever and chills, or if the symptoms last for longer than ten hours, one would add .5 gm. Sulfasuxidine tablets, taking two or three four times daily at four-hour intervals for three or four days. These sterilize the intestines of certain bacteria. They are not absorbed into the body and the general circulation, but limit their action to the intestines.

Be on the lookout for other causes of diarrhea and vomiting listed below.

● *Typhoid-Paratyphoid Organisms*

Typhoid is serious and can be fatal. Its treatment is best left in the hands of a skilled person. Recognize it by the severe systemic symptoms of headache, fever, and the patient's vague feeling of uneasiness. It does not respond to treatment methods outlined herein.

The pulse rate is low in relation to the fever. Normally the pulse will be over 90 or more, with a temperature over 100°. If a person has a pulse rate of 80 and a temperature over 101°, consider typhoid.

● *Other Causes of Abdominal Upsets*

These may be due to:

1. High altitude: This can cause vomiting.
2. Infection: Vomiting also can occur with any infection, as with flu or tonsillitis.

3. Hepatitis or yellow jaundice: The onset here is severe vomiting and temperature. The urine frequently is dark, and there may be pain in the upper right side under the ribs, often with a deep breath. After several days, the whites of the eyes have a yellow color. In more advanced states, the skin becomes yellow.

Rest is essential. Fortunately, complete recovery usually takes place, but because complete rest and laboratory work are so vital, it is best that the individual be evacuated as soon as practical. Those handling the patient must realize that the virus is transmitted via the stool and urine, and good burial of the latter two together with maintaining clean hands is essential to minimize the possibility of transmission to others.

4. Ulcers: If a person has a history of an ulcer, then develops upper abdominal pains and vomiting, an ulcer with perforation must be considered.

If a patient is squirming about, one would doubt a perforated ulcer. The symptoms of a perforated ulcer, on the other hand, are classical and unmistakable. *The person looks sick.* He hardly moves because of the pain. The abdomen is boardlike when you press on it. Take nothing by mouth. Outside help is essential.

- *Acute Abdomen*

This is an abdomen that will require surgical help and would include the perforated ulcer mentioned above, appendicitis, and any number of internal problems which are serious. The two signs to look for here are called "rebound" and "referred rebound" tenderness.

In "rebound" tenderness, a hand placed over the area of maximum tenderness on the abdomen and pressed deeply into the abdomen may cause discomfort in any number of non-serious conditions. If, however, after pushing deeply into the abdomen, the hand is quickly released with a snap-away motion to allow the abdominal wall to spring upwards, and a *severe* pain results over the area, this is "rebound" tenderness. It indicates early peritonitis and means that surgical help must be obtained.

If placing the hand as described over a *non-tender area* of the abdomen and, after pressing, again releasing it causes pain to shoot over to the tender area, this not only confirms the presence of a surgical abdomen, but it also means that things are further advanced and more serious ("referred rebound" tenderness).

Take no food or water, and no laxatives. An antibiotic by mouth may help, but do not count on it to prevent the need for surgery. Seek medical help with all speed.

● *Laxatives*

These are mentioned only to condemn them. If you already have the laxative habit, you no doubt have your own fixed ideas and help will be difficult. Constipation, especially when first leaving civilization, is a common problem, but certainly no dire consequences will result if you do not have a movement for several days. Drink adequate fluids, and things will establish themselves in due time. There is no truth to the theory of autointoxication from wastes in your system.

● *External Hemorrhoids*

Many people in good health have these, and they present themselves to a doctor fearfully, afraid they have a terrible problem. Actually, it is a common problem. It is not like *internal hemorrhoids*.

First, a painful pea-like or marble-like lump is felt in the anal area. This is tender so that, eventually, sitting may become painful. The lump is bluish-red in color. It can follow physical injury, such as that incurred from sitting down hard, straining at stool, or horseback riding.

The lump eventually will break with slow bleeding that can last two to seven days. When this happens, clean the area, take the hemostat clamp and pull out the clot which is within, to hasten healing. As long as the clot is inside the broken hemorrhoid, the bleeding will tend to persist, and healing will be retarded. Keep the diet simple while healing goes on.

### • *Hernia*

This is a tearing of the supporting structures in the groin just above and lateral to the pubic bone. It may be but a small bulge detectable only by the trained finger of a doctor, or it may be a noticeable bulge visible to the observant eye. The treatment is surgical, although the bulge can often be held back with a hand. All further straining and lifting should be avoided until the hernia can be attended to in civilization.

A hernia that cannot be reduced, which usually happens with a hernia of some duration, is always a medical emergency. If gentle, never forceful, pressure will not push the bulge back, help must be sought at once.

### • *Hiccough*

This is caused by a spasmodic contraction of the diaphragm. Some cases go on for weeks and need surgical intervention.

Hiccoughs usually can be stopped by the following methods:

1. Drink four to six ounces of ice water fast.

2. Hold breath and count as long as possible. The idea behind this is to let the carbon dioxide in the lungs build up.

3. Blow up a paper bag over the mouth. Now

rebreathe from the paper bag as much as possible. Again, the idea is to let the carbon dioxide build up.

4. With both eyes closed, press on the eyeballs firmly enough to make them uncomfortable.

The cases that do not respond usually are in older people with arteriosclerosis, or other problems. Stopping the hiccoughs can be difficult, indeed.

# 9

## INFECTIONS IN THE RESPIRATORY SYSTEM

RESPIRATORY INFECTIONS, fortunately, are uncommon in the back country and away from civilization. The first problem to decide is whether the infection needs an antibiotic at all. Perhaps simply rest, aspirin, and a light diet for a few days will suffice.

Many nose and throat infections are viral in nature and need no antibiotic. Generally, in viral infections the throat is not red. There is a watery nasal discharge, as in a cold, which later becomes thicker. There may be mild to moderate nausea and vomiting or diarrhea.

If the throat is sore but not red, and there are only cold symptoms, one would not treat with an antibiotic, even though the patient had a fever.

If there were a complicating factor such as earache, sore neck glands, or chest infection, then one would be inclined to use an antibiotic for proper treatment. While from a physician's standpoint this is not strictly true, we have to decide something—make a choice—and this is as good a rule as any.

● *Tonsillitis*

The tonsils are swollen. Often there is fever, and there may be general aching, as in flu. There may or may not be a white, patchy covering on the tonsil.

Aspirin and gargles help. Painting the throat is a barbaric medieval custom and should be abandoned; besides being uncomfortable, it is worthless as a cure.

An antibiotic should be started. This should be continued for seven to ten days, even if the symptoms have abated within a few days.

● *Strep Throat*

This usually is the same germ that causes tonsillitis. The treatment is the same. The throat is red, and swallowing is painful. Use your own eating and drinking utensils, so you do not pass this along to your friends.

● *Laryngitis*

If laryngitis comes and goes over the course of several hours, it may be nothing more than mucus on the vocal cords. The mucus arises from points higher in the throat and drains onto the cords. If this is the case, no special treatment is needed.

If the laryngitis is persistent, and has not come from voice abuse such as yelling, it probably should be treated, particularly as any extension of this further into the chest will result in bronchitis. Three or four days of an antibiotic will suffice.

● *Bronchitis*

This usually follows a cold or an inadequately treated respiratory infection. Cough is present, and the chest often hurts upon coughing or breathing. Often the breathing has a raspy sound, especially if someone listens with an ear placed on the chest.

Rest is essential. An antibiotic should be used until the symptoms abate. Usually this takes place within four days except in more severe or resistant cases. Steam inhalations may help. An aspirin with codeine tablet each four or five hours will control the hacking cough. Too, a soothing mixture often can be improvised with honey, maple syrup, jam, citric-acid crystals, or even sugar.

● *Pneumonia*

This is more serious. Fever may or *may not* be present. Each breath may be painful (pleurisy), and the sputum may be thick and may have flecks of blood or be rust-stained in appearance.

Rest is essential. Ten to fourteen days' treatment with an antibiotic is necessary. The same measures suggested for bronchitis should be used. Supporting measures, such as an ample intake of fluids and a daily vitamin tablet, are worthwhile.

Do not waste time and effort on poultices, physics, mustard plasters, chest rubs, red tape applied to the chest, ointments on the chest, and other relics of antiquity. *Do not tape or strap the chest to prevent the pain of breathing.* This is the worst thing you can do.

● *Common Cold*

This is a viral infection which lasts ten to fourteen days. A temperature may run for the first twenty-four hours, then return to normal. It is difficult to distinguish flu from many of the other associated cold viruses. A cold is nothing more than a mild flu. The temperature does not go above normal beyond twenty-four hours, and the throat, while sore, does not appear red or irritated.

Rest, reduced activity, two aspirin each four hours, and a light diet with forced fluids will suffice. There is no evidence that the use of an antibiotic shortens the course of the illness or lessens the complications.

# 10

## GETTING AHEAD OF
## HEAD PROBLEMS

THERE ARE MANY HEAD PROBLEMS that can plague
the outdoorsman in a remote area. Here we deal
with typical head problems such as headache, concussion, nosebleeds, toothache, and problems of the
ear and mouth.

● *Headache*

This is a symptom and not an illness. It can occur
with infection, injuries, indigestion, nervous tension,
tumor, and for many other reasons. The average
headache is not serious and is of short duration.
This is the one which the woodsman usually has to
concern himself about.

Aspirin or APC will handle most headaches.

Darvon Compound or aspirin with codeine, grains ½, may be used for the more severe ones.

Headache is common in some people at high altitudes before they become acclimated. APC works better than aspirin here because the caffeine in it serves to combat the often accompanying drowsiness or depression.

● *Concussion*

This is caused by a blow to the head, or it can be a result of a severe shaking motion of the head. Headache usually accompanies it. Actually, a concussion results in swelling of the brain tissue, much the way a bruise elsewhere will swell. After a severe head injury, rest is important if a concussion has occurred. The rest permits things to heal and return to normal.

Often it is asked, which is worse, a skull fracture or a concussion? Usually a concussion will accompany a skull fracture, but not always. There have been individuals with a skull fracture apparent on X-ray and no symptoms, and those with no fracture, but with considerable symptoms from the concussion. In general, though, a severe blow can cause bleeding between the skull and the brain, or into the brain, and this is the problem.

In a head injury, then, look for the danger signs. In a simple concussion, the individual has his wits about him. The headache is of short duration—one or two days. Vomiting, if present, is not there for long.

A severe injury will cause increasingly unremitting headache, some fuzziness in thinking, often violent and continuous vomiting, and sometimes a stiff neck. The pupils of the eyes may be unequal when compared in the same light. Do not try to compare them if the light is coming from one side.

Sometimes one side of the face may droop from weakness of the muscles, or an arm or leg may not work properly. There may be bleeding from the ears or mouth, or a clear, watery fluid may be dripping from the nose. These are all danger signs, and the patient must be put at rest and help sought immediately.

One thing: Let the patient sleep if he wants to. True, some people think he should be kept awake. You want to be sure, of course, that the sleep is natural, and not a coma with deep, throaty breathing, but certainly sleep otherwise is permissible.

### • Nosebleeds

Here is a subject for which nearly everyone has a favorite worthless remedy, ranging from scissors on the forehead to cold cloths on the neck. In accordance with the elsewhere discussed methods of stopping bleeding, direct pressure over the bleeding site is the thing to achieve.

Simply have the person sit upright—never let him

lie down—and squeeze the nose tightly together between the fingers, just below the nose bone which ends in the middle of the nose. Hold this for five minutes. Do not let go! This will stop over ninety-five per cent of all nosebleeds.

Occasionally the bleeding is high in the nose above the bone level. This type of bleeding usually occurs in the aged and in those with high blood pressure. It may or may not stop spontaneously. Fortunately, it is rarely encountered in outdoorsmen. In the case of very high bleeding above the area which can be compressed, cold is worth trying, but it still is a third-rate remedy.

Bleeding from a fractured nose usually will stop of its own accord. Remember to keep the patient sitting up. In the case of high nosebleeds, as in fracture and other causes, cold compresses on the back of the neck may be of some help.

After the bleeding is controlled in any event, it is a good idea to keep vaseline or a similar bland ointment inside the nose on the septum (mid-portion) for a few days to prevent the scab over the bleeding site from breaking loose prematurely and bleeding again.


● *Bugs and Other Foreign Material in Ears*


The only serious offender is the Japanese beetle, common in the eastern United States and Canada. This culprit can chew through the eardrum in a matter of minutes. Other bugs are a nuisance, but they often can be removed with a cotton-covered swab.

When inserting anything into the ear, always pull the earlobe back until it is uncomfortable. This straightens the canal and makes whatever has to be done easier. By doing this it is possible to see right down to the drum with a good light. Try it! The drum appears as a gray window shade across the canal.

Often a bug or other foreign object can be removed with the hemostat or tweezers under direct vision. If a cotton applicator is used, leave a little fuzz on the end by teasing some of the end-cotton loose to form whiskers. Then slowly insert with a slight twisting motion, all the time holding the earlobe back.

When the drum is touched, there will be a slight tickling sensation, followed by a desire to cough. Now withdraw, making pressure against the sides of the canal.

If these measures fail, the ear can be irrigated by flushing the canal with a syringe of lukewarm water, or by simply flooding the ear with mineral oil or clean cooking oil. Always inquire before doing this, though, to be sure the individual does not have a history of a perforated eardrum. It is logical that we would not want such substances to go through a chronic hole in the drum into the delicate inner ear chamber.

● *Earaches*

These are due to an infection in the ear canal, an infection of the eardrum (middle-ear infection or *otitis media*), or from referred pain emanating actually not from the ear at all. A case of tonsillitis or an impacted wisdom tooth can cause ear pain even though there is nothing at all wrong with the ear itself. If such is the case, treatment must be directed not to the ear, but to the real cause.

Ordinarily, it is easy to differentiate between the serious middle-ear infection and the not-so-serious yet uncomfortable ear canal infection. You have been told that pulling the earlobe back straightens the canal so that it is possible, using a good light, to see the eardrum itself. If pulling the earlobe back produces pain, most likely you are confronted with a canal infection, the painful ear reacting much the same as would the skin if pulled taut over a boil. On the other hand, if pulling the earlobe back registers little discomfort, the problem is a middle-ear infection.

One word of caution now! If the primary affliction really is a ruptured eardrum, you could mistakenly think it merely a canal infection. Here's why. A ruptured eardrum produces drainage moving out into the canal. While associated with this drainage will be the same painful ear reaction common to simple canal infections when the earlobe is pulled, you must not too quickly decide that this is all there is to the problem. In such a case, what appears to be merely a canal infection might well be only a subordinate affliction; an underlying eardrum or middle-ear infection might well be the real problem. See next topic.

● *Middle-Ear Infections*

A middle-ear infection often is accompanied by fever, and usually there is a history of a cold or sore throat within the past week. Hearing is decreased because the drum is swollen.

The infection should be treated for one week with an antibiotic. (See section on antibiotics in chapter 17.) If the ear is draining, the canal should be wiped clean frequently. A draining ear must always be treated three or four days beyond the time it becomes dry. This is minimum.

It is impracticable to carry ear drops into remote areas, and ordinarily these are not necessary if an antibiotic is taken by mouth. Do not put other things into the ear, although the pain of the acute phase often can be relieved by instilling warm oil in the ear. Again, never do this if the drum has ruptured.

Ten grains of aspirin every three or four hours helps pain, or Darvon Compound or aspirin with codeine can be used if relief still is needed.

## • External Ear Canal Infection

Here the canal is swollen and painful, and the inner ear is not involved. Usually it results from water being left in an ear following showering or swimming. Often no treatment is necessary except aspirin for pain relief.

In the more severe cases, even fever may result, and the whole canal may be swollen shut. Three to four days of an oral antibiotic should be used, and the antibiotic eye ointment described elsewhere can be instilled into the ear without difficulty three to four times daily. The small tip on the container of the antibiotic eye ointment is just right for ear installation.

## • Eustachian Tube Pain

Often the ear will click and pop, especially after a cold or after one has descended from a high altitude. This usually is self-limiting, although it may take several to ten days.

An antihistamine, such as 50 mg. of Pyribenzamine every four hours, helps. This should be continued until the condition remedies itself, usually in six to ten days. Steam inhalations help, too. The ear feels stopped up. It usually is possible to clear it by pinching the nose and blowing slightly with the mouth closed.

● *Toothache*

This usually is due to a small abscess at the base of a cavity. If the cavity can be identified, clean it out as thoroughly as possible with a sharp point and pack a small amount of oil of cloves into it. Take aspirin or a stronger pain remedy, such as Darvon Compound or Emperin with codeine, by mouth. It is a good idea to take an antibiotic for three or four days, or, if the jaw is swollen, until the swelling subsides.

● *Loss of an Inlay*

For those fortunate enough to have inlays and unfortunate enough to lose one, a temporary filling can be made by mixing equal parts of zinc oxide and Eugenol. Mix well and pack into the hole.

● *Gum Trouble—Gingivitis*

Almost always this occurs from improper brushing of the teeth. The gums are swollen, red, and painful. Take an antibiotic for three or four days until the inflammation subsides, and then resume brushing the teeth several times daily. If toothpaste is not available, use plain baking soda.

● *Mouth Blisters*

An outbreak of small and large fever blisters on the inside of the mouth is called aphthous stomatitis. It may be accompanied by fever as high as 104°. The mouth is inflamed, and the membranes, gums, tongue, and even the throat may develop many blisters and ulcers.

This lasts one week with treatment, and seven days without treatment. But, although it is self-limiting, it may be contagious so others should not use the same eating and drinking utensils. An antibiotic is of no help, so do not use one.

# 11

## YOUR EYES IN THE
## FAR COUNTRY

GOOD VISION is always an asset but of almost paramount importance to the outdoorsman. Here we treat the various eye ailments which can handicap a bush-country traveler badly such as conjunctivitis, various eye infections and injuries, sties and chalazion, and the problem of foreign bodies in the eye.

• *Conjunctivitis*

Conjunctivitis results from infection or irritation. The white of the eye is red, and it often feels as though there is something in the eye. It can follow the presence of a small foreign body in the eye, and long after the object is removed the eye feels as though the object is still there.

When there is an infection, it is called "pink eye."

With infection there frequently is matter in the eye, especially in the morning upon arising. Too much sunlight, particularly in the high altitudes in snow, can cause tearing of the eyes and redness. This also is a conjunctivitis, but there is no infection.

If there is infection, an antibiotic ointment such as Spectrocin Ophthalmic Ointment can be used each four hours. Never squirt eye medication directly into the eye. The correct way is to pull down the lower lid. When the lid is released, the medicine will be carried onto the surface of the eye. Keeping the eye closed for a few minutes afterward helps. This medication should be carried out for three to five days, until the infection is under control and the eye appears normal.

If the eye is only irritated, then Butyn or Metycaine eye ointment will give relief. Even better, if carrying liquids is no problem, is a mixture of Pontocaine and Neohydeltrasol, mixed in equal parts. This is a local anaesthetic for the eye, plus a Neomycin-Cortisone mixture for the treatment of infection or inflammation of the eyes. This is the thing to use if the eye is hit by a flying chip of wood or anything similar. One drop each three hours suffices. It also will give immediate relief in snow blindness, often suffered at high altitudes.

Because the Pontocaine anaesthetizes the eye, and the eye loses its protective wink reflexes, stay out of windy places after using it. Better yet, wear a patch over the eye for two hours after putting in the drops. Their effect is about gone by then. Wearing glasses also helps. Incidentally, the same precautions are advisable with Butyn or Metycaine ointments.

Additional measures for eye discomfort are two aspirin or a Darvon Compound capsule for relief of discomfort, and cold compresses.

● *Superficial and Deep Eye Infections*

We have been talking about infections that involve the *conjunctiva* or outer covering of the eye. Deep infections are much more serious, can result in blindness, and *must* have professional attention. Below is a table comparing the differences.

| *Superficial* | *Deep Infection* |
|---|---|
| Pupil round and regular. | Pupil irregular. |
| Pupil reacts to light shone in the eye by switching a light off and on. | Pupil sluggish or showing no response to light. |
| Redness of eye white mainly confined to outer portion. | Eye red, or redder, about or near the pupil. |
| The pupil is clear. | Pupil has a steamy appearance. |

The pupil, of course, is the hole in the eye in the center of the iris or colored part of the eye. It is black.

If a deep infection is present, start an antibiotic such as Erythromycin in full dosage, put a patch over the eye to cover it and to prevent its use, and find professional help or face *possible blindness*.

● *Eye Injuries*

Again, these have a serious potential and need skilled help. Always put both eyes at rest. One eye can not rest if the other moves about. Put patches over both eyes, start an antibiotic, and control pain with Darvon Compound or codeine.

● *Corneal Abrasions*

This is a scratch on the membrane covering the eye. It feels as though something is in the eye. It can be seen usually only with a special stain, but if nothing is seen in the eye after careful inspection (see Foreign Bodies next), it is most likely that a scratch has occurred.

Use a little of the anaesthetic ointment or liquid if the discomfort is great or if it cannot be controlled by aspirin or one of the other pain tablets. It is best not to use an anaesthetic unless it is absolutely necessary. It is surprising how the underestimated aspirin is so useful in a situation such as this, as well as on any of the surface outer coverings of the body: eyes, ears, teeth, skin burns, itch, etc. Also put in a little of the Spectrocin ointment, cover the eye, and it will be well or improved by the next day or after a night's rest.

● *Foreign Bodies in the Eye*

Most people are familiar with this problem, but here are a few comments. First, get a *good* light. Have the patient fix his eye straight ahead and not roll it about. Do not attempt to find the object through his telling you where he thinks it is!

Now look at the eye to get the general picture. If nothing is seen, pull the lower lid down and look there while the person looks up. Now have him look to the right, then to the left, and then up and down, while you try to spot something on the surface of the eye. Do not confuse a fleck with the speckles on the colored iris about the pupil. Looking from the side across the eye with a light over the looker's shoulder often discloses an otherwise missed foreign body.

Now lift up the upper lid by having the patient look down, grasping the eyelashes, and pulling the eyelid up over a wooden match. Note that the lid is not rolled up, but is folded up over the match.

If a fleck of dirt is seen, flick it off cleanly with a corner of a handkerchief. Do not smear or wipe it off, for then a corneal abrasion will certainly result.

If nothing is seen, flooding the eye with copious amounts of water sometimes will bring the object into view for a repeated inspection. If still nothing is seen, stop right there. It may be one of the causes already mentioned, such as infection, or an abrasion, or a chalazion. (See next topic.) Put a little anaesthetic ointment or liquid in the eye, take aspirin, and see what develops. Cover the eye if a branch or some other object hits it. Assume an abrasion is present and treat accordingly.

If the object is seen but will not flick out, then we have an imbedded foreign body in the cornea. Removing it will take some doing, but it really is not complicated. First, have the individual lie down, with his head supported so it doesn't bounce around. Use some anaesthetic in the lower lid and wait five minutes.

In the meantime, find the 11 Bard-Parker scalpel blade and have it in readiness. Approach the eye from a tangent, never with the tip of the blade pointed down toward the eyeball. Simply flick out the foreign body. The worst problem is a piece of metal that has been in the eye for a day or so. There is rust about it, and repeated attempts may be required to get the area clean.

● *Sties and Chalazia*

These are noteworthy because when they are starting, they simulate the discomfort of a foreign body. Many people who think something might be in the eye in reality have one of these mischievous afflictions.

A stye is simply a small pimple at the eyelid margin in the area of a hair follicle. A chalazion is an infection in one of the lubricating glands beneath the lid. Both start with a scratchy feeling, and the lid may become swollen and irritated.

The stye can be opened by lifting off the head when it is ripe. The chalazion eventually will rupture. In the backwoods, nothing need be done except to use some antibiotic ointment to keep the rest of the eye from becoming infected. Chalazia tend to reoccur, and their ultimate prevention can be attended to when back in civilization. Aside from the discomfort they cause, they are self-limiting.

# 12

## FISHHOOKS, BLISTERS, BURNS, SPECIAL PROBLEMS

WHAT WE ARE PRONE to think of often as small problems can sometimes suddenly reach acute stages to the point of incapacitating a man in the Far Country. This chapter covers a number in that category including some that can be avoided. Here we deal with joint inflammations such as bursitis, and problems such as those occasioned by blisters, burns, fishhooks stuck in the skin, those caused by splinters or thorns, and some presented by ingrown nails together with allied infections.

* *Bursitis*

A bursa is a mucous membrane sheath which surrounds tendons and joints. It acts as a lubricating sleeve where tendons pass over bony prominences, such as the tip of the shoulder or the elbow. If this becomes inflamed, it is painful, and the use of the involved part is limited.

In the shoulder, it commonly occurs after a repetitive action such as chopping wood or paddling a canoe. The repeated action of a given set of muscles which are not in condition causes the bursa to become inflamed, and any movement of the joint beyond a small range is painful. For example, it often is impossible to raise the arm beyond fifteen degrees from the side.

Recovery is one thing that cannot be hurried. Rest and a sling to limit use, in the case of an arm, is essential for a speedy restoration. Depending on the inflammation's severity, recovery will occur in forty-eight hours to ten days. Aspirin at regular four-hour intervals helps. (See Cortisone, chapter 17.)

There also is a bursa of the knee and the elbow. These joints can swell visibly. The trouble is caused by a considerable collection of fluid. Kneeling for an extended period, as in a canoe, or hammering are common causes.

● *Tenosynovitis*

This is like bursitis. It usually occurs in the lower forearm muscles or in the leg, and any motion is painful because the sheath through which the tendon slips is inflamed. Bursitis and tenosynovitis are described because they are not at all uncommon in individuals taking up a new outdoor activity, and they can be quite disabling. Treatment, again, is rest. (Also, see Cortisone, chapter 17.)

## • *Ingrown Toenails*

Ingrown toenails invariably result from improper cutting of the toenails. Always cut straight across; never round the edges.

Once a nail becomes ingrown, the individual sometimes attempts to dig the nail free by cutting

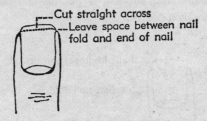

Cut straight across
Leave space between nail fold and end of nail

**Cut Nails Properly**

**Alternate Nail-Cutting Method**

For incipient ingrown nail, or those with a tendency to ingrow.

[ 119 ]

even more of it. Next, it becomes infected, and one has a mess.

Cut your nails correctly, and if ingrowing does occur, soak the foot for twenty minutes in warm water four to six times daily. Make an attempt to cut a deep central V in the nail, as shown in the illustration. Stay away from the corners of the nail.

Tape applied to the edge of the affected skin, and under and around the toe, helps to pull the flesh away from the nail for relief. In persistent problems, the affected half of the nail is removed all the way to the nail base, but this is painful and should be done only by a doctor.

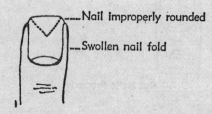

**Exaggerated "V" Cut in Case of Ingrown Nail**

**Taping to Pull Fold Away from Nail for Symptomatic Relief**

**Infected Hangnail (Paronychia)**
**Key to drawing:**
x x x—Swollen nail fold from infection
· · · · · ·—Line of incision (hockey stick)
To relieve pus, incise over area of greatest swelling.

## • *Infected Hangnail*

With infected hangnail, called *paronychia,* the skin about the base of the fingernail and along its side becomes swollen, red, and eventually softened with pus. When it becomes ripe with pus, it should be opened, as shown in the illustration. Its ripening can be hastened by hot soaks four to six times daily for twenty minutes each.

Prior to opening, the sensation can be deadened by soaking in water as close to freezing as possible (ice cubes in a jar of fresh water) for ten minutes. There is no relieving it except by opening it because the finger will continue tense and throbbing.

## • *Felon*

Here is a more serious situation. It usually follows a puncture wound of the tip of the finger which then becomes infected. Pus forms in the pocket at the end of the finger, next to the end of the bone. If the pus is not relieved, the bone itself will become infected, with possible loss of the finger.

The finger is anaesthetized with ice-cold fresh water, as previously described, and the area opened as shown. Antibiotics cannot be relied on to control infection, but nevertheless should be used as an adjunct to opening the infection. An 11 Bard-Parker scalpel blade does the job easily. This is not a pleasant procedure to undergo, but neglect will cause even more unpleasantness.

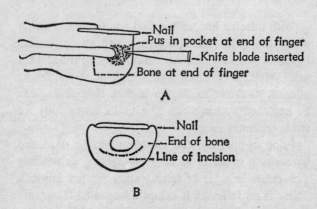

A

B

**Treatment of Felon**

A. Side view of felon to show depth of incision.   B. End view of finger to show "fish mouth" type incision.

● *Blisters*

These should never happen in the first place. Gear should be well broken in before the big trip beyond, socks changed frequently, feet kept clean and dry, and any sensitive spots protected, if they develop, with little adhesive bandages.

If a blister still should form, leave it alone. The best sterile dressing is the covering that nature put over it; therefore it should not be opened. If it should break spontaneously, trim off the dead skin with manicure scissors, apply a little antibiotic ointment such as Baciguent, and keep dressed until new skin grows over.

Keep Merthiolate and alcohol off open blisters. Clean them instead with soap and water. Alcohol and Merthiolate are skin disinfectants, not *wound* disinfectants. They kill delicate tissue, and while reducing the germ count initially, they harm the tissue. Germs multiply best on injured tissues, so you see you actually foster infection rather than reduce it with the use of these so-called disinfectants. Soap and water are best for cleansing a wound.

● *Fishhooks*

If the hook is imbedded in the skin beyond the barb, it is best to push it all the way through rather than attempt to pull it out. The shank is cut off and the hook is pushed through, or the barb is clipped off, and the hook is pulled back whence it came.

● *Burns*

If a blister should form from a burn, it should be left alone, as with ordinary blisters. A first-degree burn requires little treatment. Only the skin will become red. As pointed out, aspirin relieves the sting of a burn. Ointments are messy and do little good.

A second-degree burn involves blistering or the loss of some of the top skin. Vaseline makes a soothing dressing. Sterilize this by melting and bringing it to the boiling point, then allowing it to cool. Apply to gauze flats or some other dressing material by buttering, as on a piece of bread. This is preferable to attempting to spread it on the burn and then covering with gauze.

Third-degree burns are nasty at best. The skin is burned all the way through, and the area either will have to be grafted on or granulated in from the sides. As described under Loss of Tip of Finger, chapter 2, this can cause severe scarring and take weeks to mend.

● *Splinters and Thorns*

Everyone knows about these. Be radical with slivers under the nail. Most people keep nipping at the splinter and cutting the nail back as they go. Each time they cut the nail back a little, they chew off a little from the end of the splinter and are no further along than when they started.

It is essential that the nail be cut back in a V over the splinter, well back of its end, so a good grasp can be secured. The Mosquito hemostat works well for this. Ordinary nail clippers are superior to scissors in cutting the nail back.

● *Blood Under Nail*

The pressure of blood under a nail, resulting from jamming a finger or dropping something on a foot, is a common if minor source of discomfort. These can be opened to drain the blood and relieve the pressure by twirling the point of the 11 Bard-Parker scalpel blade over the center of the nail discoloration until blood seeps out the hole. If you're away from camp and your medical kit, a pointed knife will do instead.

Because the nail is lifted by the blood, there is no danger of drilling into the flesh if you take it easy. It takes only gentle pressure while twirling the steel to drill the nail. Let the point do the work, and do not push hard on the blade.

# 13

## KIDNEY STONES AND AILMENTS OF THE LOWER REGION

THIS CHAPTER treats kidney or bladder infections, kidney stones, epididymitis, and problems occasioned by a severe blow to the testes.

● *Kidney or Bladder Infections*

An infection of the kidney or bladder is commonly accompanied by cloudy urine, often bloody, and by frequency and burning of urination. No sooner is the bladder emptied when the desire to empty it again occurs. even though it contains very little.

In a kidney infection, there is tenderness in the flank over the involved kidney. This is not the back pain which so often follows a sprain and which many people are sure stems from their kidneys. This pain is well out in the flanks.

A bladder infection causes discomfort to pressure over the bladder area. A prostate infection may be deeper toward the bowel. Fever, headache, and general muscular aching may be present.

For relief of the burning and frequency, take one Pyridium each three to four hours, as needed. This cures nothing, but it causes a gratifying relief of symptoms. It turns the urine orange.

For the infection, take the Gantrisin (sulfa) tablets four times daily for one week. Do not stop when feeling better. A supply of fifty Gantrisin tablets is a wise measure in a well-rounded outdoor medical chest. (Eighteen Pyridium tablets should also suffice.) This should take care of the average infection.

Of course, there are some germs that will not respond to the sulfa (Gantrisin), and there are those people who have a chronic recurrent problem in need of a formal medical work-up. But for the individual who is the chance victim of an attack, this is the thing to do. Infections are more common in women than in men.

The Gantrisin also can be used in a pinch for pneumonia or other bacterial infections if the Erythromycin happens to be used up, but it is not as effective as Erythromycin, hence not the number one drug of choice in infections other than urinary tract infections.

● *Kidney Stone*

The pain is severe, often responding only to morphine. It characteristically radiates down from the side of the involved kidney into the scrotum, although there may be variations to this. There are periods of freedom from pain when the stone is not moving.

Fortunately, this is an uncommon problem, but it is mentioned for the sake of completeness. If you should be unlucky enough to have one, drink copious amounts of water in the hope of flushing the stone free. Naturally, an accurate evaluation depends on X-ray and other tests, so a doctor should be seen as soon as practical.

● *Epididymitis*

This, the swelling of the cap over the testis, is a very common problem in healthy males. It usually starts on one side. Then the other side also may become involved, but not always. The testicle is swollen and painful, and there may be a fever. It can result from an infection or a bruise.

Treatment involves rest until the swelling goes down, which may be five days to five weeks. It you must be on your feet, a scrotal support, such as the brief-type underwear, will help. An antibiotic should be used for a week to see if it has a helpful effect. Often it does not. Bed rest is essential for a speedy recovery. Heat or ice are not especially used in treatment.

● *Blows to the Testes*

Using ice compresses to minimize swelling, bed rest until the swelling subsides, and Darvon Compound for the relief of pain is the best approach here.

# 14

## KNOCKED OUT BY HEAT OR COLD

THE BEST PRESCRIPTION is prevention in the first place!

● *Chilblains*

Prolonged exposure to dry cold may cause the skin to redden, swell, and become somewhat tender with itching. The condition is mild, but uncomfortable. No treatment is indicated, although a bland ointment, such as zinc-oxide or even vaseline, helps.

● *Frostbite*

Frostbite is indicated by a sudden blanching of the skin on the nose, ear, cheek, etc., accompanied by a tingling sensation. The skin has a yellow-white appearance, or a yellow-white spot appears which is best detected by a companion. The Buddy system is a good one—watch your companion for the first sign of frostbite.

Next, feeling decreases. If there is no longer any pain or discomfort, stop and check. The frostbitten skin will be cold and frosty, and it will have a crisp or resilient feel. This is in contradiction to deep frostbite where there is ice in the tissues beneath the skin and when they have a wooden feeling.

The best treatment is quick thawing in a water bath of 102°. This water should be warm, *but not hot,* to the touch. In the field, a bared hand can be held over the face until the latter hurts again, a foot thawed on a friend's stomach, or a hand put in your warm armpit.

● *Deep Freezing*

Deep freezing is much more serious. Gangrene and loss of skin or digits and extremities can result. Prevent by avoiding excess fatigue, alcohol, and by eating hot meals and wearing proper clothing.

Here the skin is yellow-white, but it will not roll over bony prominences. It is painless and wooden. Indoors, droplets of water condense or sweat on it as on a glass of ice water in the summer.

Take warm drinks, if possible, to raise the output

of body heat. Rewarm rapidly, never slowly. Never rub with snow. It is important, too, to seek any available help before thawing.

If there is no help, wait until you reach camp to thaw. No harm will be done if you wait four to eight hours before thawing the area. On the other hand, gangrene and other problems will almost surely follow if the area is thawed either by a well-meaning friend or by accident, and then refrozen. The gangrene then will occur in four to seven days.

The thawed area is subject to infection, too— another reason why it is better not to thaw it until conditions are better than on the trail. Everything in contact with the thawed area, such as clothing, or a splint if any extremity also happens to be broken, should be loose. There never should be any snug bandages.

It is better to walk for miles on a frozen extremity than to attempt to thaw it spontaneously. If it does thaw spontaneously, bandage loosely and with large amounts of fluffy bandages, simply loosening gauze flats by shaking them out to make a fluffy dressing. Take no alcohol. Again, rapid rewarming is a specific treatment and minimizes future tissue loss and tissue damage. Rewarm in a container of water at 102°— again, never hot. Be extremely careful if using dry heat as from a campfire, as a burn can be easily superimposed on an already injured tissue.

Thawing may take up to an hour. It should be continued until all blueness and paleness turns to pink or burgundy red. If the part is already thawed, however, do not rewarm.

The area must now be protected from infection until the skin is dry and free from blisters or weeping. Blisters invariably complicate freezing. Clear blisters near the ends of the extremities often are a good sign, but blood-filled ones and those higher on the extremity are an indication that there is danger of losing the extremity.

Never break the blisters. Leave them alone. In camp, keep from infection by using sterile dressings. A clean towel which is boiled for ten minutes, then dried, should do. Wrap lightly. Tetanus should be no problem if the individual has brought his tetanus shots up to date before going afield.

Put the joints through a range of motion ten minutes twice daily in 94° water baths, which should also help to keep the area cleansed.

Often there is much anxiety and fear at the time thawing initiates. Pain tablets or capsules, such as Darvon Compound, should be administered. Proceed with the thawing, in any event, regardless of pain or reluctance on the part of the patient to follow it through.

The extremity may demarcate itself and spontaneously amputate itself in time. Remember that color of skin and skin loss below the line of demarcation, which will develop to separate normal from abnormal skin, is no indication of the end result.

Smoking is to be discouraged. Amputations by a

doctor should be delayed at least three months. In short, with deep freezing the results may be serious.

● *Trench Foot*

Trench foot is caused by prolonged immersion of the foot in water or by having wet feet for hours in temperatures above freezing. The foot first becomes cold and has a mottled appearance. Later it gets red and swollen and is warm.

Disability may last for years, with swollen feet, burning discomfort, and sensitivity to cold. Beware of thermal boots and water-tight boots in which the feet are constantly bathed in their own perspiration.

● *Immersion in Cold Water*

The amount and kind of clothing worn controls the rapidity with which the body loses heat. In water close to freezing, there is an initial shock which takes the breath away, then shivering, followed by very rapid loss of voluntary control of hands and muscles. Consciousness lasts four to seven minutes, and death occurs in fifteen to twenty minutes. A few can save themselves by violent exertion until they can reach shore or be pulled out. Violent exertion seems to decrease the rapidity with which the body temperature is lowered.

Contrariwise, it is best to exert oneself as little as possible in water over 45°. Treatment consists of artificial respiration if the person is not breathing, and warming in a tub of water at 106°, if possible, or by putting the patient in a sleeping bag and using hot rocks, canteens, etc., to warm him.

● *Frozen Lungs*

These are due to breathing and exertion in very cold air, twenty or more degrees below zero. This causes coughing of blood, burning in the chest, and asthma-like breathing for several hours. The lungs are not actually frozen. Treatment consists of steam inhalations, rest, and no smoking. Things subside in a day or so. Prevent by using face mufflers, etc.

● *Heat Exhaustion*

Heat exhaustion occurs among those who exert themselves in an excessively warm environment, such as in the desert. There may be weakness and dizziness, or headache for several days. Often there is fainting. Sweating may be profuse at first. Before collapsing, the patient becomes weak, pale, and clammy.

The body temperature is normal or subnormal. If the latter, use hot packs. Recovery is the rule. Rest in a cooler location is the treatment. Salt is not especially indicated, but it does no harm together with copious fluids.

● *Heat Stroke*

Heat stroke is *entirely different* from heat exhaustion. The result is often fatal. In this condition, the body temperature rises, often as high as 112°. The skin is hot and dry. It is imperative that the body temperature be lowered.

The onset is sudden, although it may be preceded by dizziness, nausea, and vomiting.

These patients are not dehydrated but are suffering primarily from a failure of the circulation and the body's heat-regulatory mechanism. Treatment consists of removal to a cool spot and, if possible, cool baths or rubdowns. Do not ordinarily use ice, as this may force the blood into the body away from the skin, thereby further increasing the body temperature. If ice is used, then the extremities of the body must be vigorously massaged to keep the circulation going while the ice packs are in progress. Unlike heat exhaustion, heat stroke is a serious condition and medical help must be sought.

Often patients who have suffered from heat exhaustion and heat stroke become so vulnerable to recurrence of these maladies that they must stay away from hot climates. Heat stroke is seen most often in those in poor physical condition and in the aged, but it can occur to anyone.

## • Heat Cramps

Heat cramps occur from excessive sweating and inadequate amount of sodium (salt). They usually are aggravated by drinking excessive amounts of water, as you can very easily do in hot mountain country, without a sufficient salt intake. Ordinary table-salt tablets can be purchased by those hiking and perspiring profusely in warm environments.

The onset of heat cramps may be heralded by muscular twitching and nausea. There is dizziness, and the skin is wet. Violent cramps may seize the individual in the upper abdominal muscles and also may occur in an arm or leg.

Treatment consists of rest in a cool area and the ingestion of sufficient salt. The idea that sugar helps is fallacious.

# 15

## SHOCK—LIFE-SAVING METHODS

THIS CHAPTER covers several emergencies requiring artificial respiration, the problems occasioned by high altitude, diabetes, insulin shock, and epilepsy.

• *Shock*

Shock may be immediate, or it may be delayed for several hours after its incitement. Usually it follows a severe injury, blow, or fracture. It may be induced by such circumstances as rough handling, cold, severe pain, or hemorrhage, particularly when the loss of blood is excessive. The skin is cold and clammy, and the patient feels light-headed and faint. The pulse is rapid, over ninety mostly, and not strong.

Treatment must be directed at the cause. Lowering the head below the level of the heart and raising the feet helps. Use a sleeping bag, blankets, or other means to promote warmth. Control pain with codeine. Avoid further movement or manipulation until the patient stabilizes himself. Often the shock can be more of a problem than the original injury.

- *Breath Stoppage—Arm Lift/Pressure Artificial Respiration*

Immediate action is necessary whenever breathing stops as a result of drowning, smoke inhalation, or electric shock as from lightning.

Check the mouth and make sure the air passage from the mouth and nose to the lungs is not blocked. Remove mucus, water, etc. If the tongue has been swallowed or is stopping the throat, hook it free with a forefinger.

Place the victim face downwards, with feet higher than the head. Loosen clothing. With the patient's elbows bent, place his hands one atop the other and under his head. Turn his face to one side, chin up, resting his cheek upon his hands.

Kneel on one or both knees at the victim's head, facing him. Place the heels of your hands just below the line between his armpits, thumb tips touching, fingers downwards and outward.

Rock forward on straight elbows, with steady pressure on the victim's back, then rock backward, sliding your hands to the other's arms just above his elbows. Grasp his arms, continuing to rock backward. Raise the arms until tension is felt, then lower them.

This completes a cycle, which should be repeated twelve times a minute, for several hours if necessary. If the victim starts to breathe of his own accord, adjust your timing to his. Once the victim has been revived, treat for shock. If possible, keep the victim lying comfortably in a quiet and warm place for twenty-four hours.

If this method does not seem to be working, mouth-to-mouth respiration must be resorted to.

● *Mouth-to-Mouth Respiration*

This is currently *believed to be superior* to any other method, especially if there is chest damage or if the surroundings are such that other methods cannot be used. It is not pleasant, but it often will save a life.

Lay the victim on his back. Clear his mouth as previously described. Pull his chin upward until the head is fully tipped back.

Now place your mouth solidly over the victim's mouth. Pinch his nostrils shut. Exhale sharply. With a small child, place your mouth over both his nose and mouth while blowing. The chest of the victim should expand during this procedure.

Good skin color and adequate chest motion will show whether the procedure is effective. A blue cast to the skin and failure of the chest to move point to an immediate need to re-check the victim's head and jaw position. His tongue may be blocking the air passage. If you still get no chest action, turn him on his side and slap him sharply several times between the shoulder blades in an effort to dislodge any foreign matter in the throat. If the victim is a child, hold him momentarily head downward while you do this. Wipe the mouth clean and resume the mouth-to-mouth breathing.

With adults, blow one vigorous breath twelve times a minute. For small children, blow shallow breaths twenty times a minute. *Don't give up* until the victim begins to breathe. Success sometimes requires hours of artificial respiration.

## • Closed Chest Cardiac Massage

If there is heart stoppage from drowning, shock, insect bite, a blow on the chest, electrocution as from lightning, or other cause, there will be: no pulse, dilated pupils, and shallow or no breathing, usually the latter.

Place the victim on his back on a firm support. Ideally, someone should give mouth-to-mouth resuscitation, while another individual is summoning the fire department or a resuscitation squad, then a doctor. In the wilderness where no help is available, naturally you will do the best you can.

Put the heel of one hand on the lower one-third of the breast bone (the sternum). Place the second hand over the first. Depress the chest. The sternum should move about an inch or an inch-and-a-quarter.

Exert your body weight straight down, not toward the abdomen or the upper chest. Do this forty to sixty times a minute while, if possible, a companion gives mouth-to-mouth resuscitation.

Check the eyes periodically. If circulation is adequate, the pupils will begin to get smaller. Also check the pulse for a readily discernible beat, and check to see if breathing has started.

If breathing and the pulse start, watch closely for the next twenty-four hours. It may be necessary to do this again as the need arises. If the pulse has not started and signs of death become apparent (dilated pupils and no circulation), then further attempts will be useless. As long as the pupils are not dilated there is yet hope, and the procedure should be continued.

• *High-Altitude Problems*

The problems peculiar to high altitude all stem from anoxia, which is a shortage of oxygen. As one ascends, there is less and less oxygen in the air and the hemoglobin in the bloodstream is no longer able to carry a full complement. At 28,000 feet, even when breathing pure oxygen we are incapable of carrying a full amount of it to the tissues. This oxygen shortage results in certain symptoms. Sometimes these are in the nature of headache and pulmonary edema with its hacking cough, but these have been discussed in chapters 10 and 6, respectively.

With slow ascents, there is acclimatization which minimizes the symptoms. Rapid ascent in an airplane, or travel via an airplane into a high remote area, can result in the symptoms of an ailment known as mountain sickness.

We are all familiar with the shortness of breath that occurs with exertion and the dizzy feeling that goes with it. At higher altitudes, especially if the ascent is made rapidly, more serious symptoms occur. The breathing may speed up for short periods and then cease for five to fifteen seconds. There may be weakness of the muscles, loss of good judgment, mental dullness, and headache. One common and dangerous effect is the development of fixed ideas which may lead to foolhardy actions. In serious cases, it may be necessary to descend to lower altitudes. Insomnia, loss of appetite, and a "don't care" attitude are common.

● *Diabetes and Insulin Shock*

Diabetic coma is due to an insufficient amount of insulin usually brought on by some acute infection or injury which increases the body's need for insulin. It generally comes on slowly.

The patient usually stays in coma. The skin is dry, and the breathing is labored. The breath has a fruity odor. The urine tastes sweet—a drop of urine on the finger to taste may not be very aesthetic, but it will do the taster no harm. Diabetic coma is always serious. Professional help must be sought.

Insulin shock is due to a lowering of the blood sugar because of too much insulin, or not enough blood sugar, so the individual passes out. The remedy for insulin shock is sugar in any form: orange juice, honey, chocolate candy, or just plain table sugar. Never give anything by mouth to a person who is unconscious, of course. The person with insulin shock should be kept warm, and he usually will come around shortly to where it is safe to give him something by mouth.

An insulin reaction usually comes on rapidly. The individual may feel faint and giddy and then pass out. His skin may be cool and clammy. His breathing is shallow. Unlike diabetic coma, there is no fruity odor to the breath. Insulin shock, while alarming in appearance, is easily combated with reduction in the amount of the patient's daily insulin dosage and by increasing the dietary allowance of food. It is self-limited. No evacuation is necessary.

● *Epilepsy*

Epilepsy can take many forms, but because of the social stigma of epilepsy it may be kept a secret from other members of the party. Briefly, epilepsy can be manifested by anything from a nodding of the head as if the person has fallen asleep for a second or two, or even a hesitation of speech in the middle of a conversation with an accompanying blank stare before the conversation is resumed, to a twitching of one extremity or a generalized convulsion.

In the event of a convulsion, the individual falls to the ground, and must be protected against biting himself. A stick wrapped in a handkerchief or shirt-tail and inserted across the mouth will prevent the individual's biting himself until the attack is spent. Several attacks may occur in succession. After a full-blown seizure the individual has a desire to rest.

Mild sedation helps. If the person does not have any special medicine with him, the use of Compazine each four hours will help, but there are much better drugs designed specifically for epilepsy. These, however, are beyond the scope of this manual.

# 16

## ANIMAL, SNAKE, SPIDER, AND TICK BITES

WHILE FORTUNATELY the problems of animal, reptile, and serious insect bite tend to be infrequent, they can present the gravest danger in certain circumstances. Every outdoorsman should therefore be familiar with the proper courses of action to be taken in each of several contingencies.

• *Poisonous Snakes*

Rattlesnakes, copperheads, coral snakes, and water moccasins are poisonous, and their bites are dangerous. Identification of the snake, therefore, is important. Strange as it may seem, many think they are bitten when they aren't. Perhaps an insect sting made them look down, and they saw the snake. Or, in jumping back from a snake, possibly the leg was pierced by a thorn or branch.

A double row of tooth marks and no fang marks are signs of a bite by a non-poisonous snake. Treat as with any puncture wound. Watch for infection and prevent tetanus.

The first symptom of bites by poisonous snakes is a feeling of stinging pain from one or two small puncture wounds in the part struck. Swelling and discoloration are evident in a very brief time. The part becomes painful. As the posion enters the system, general symptoms develop, such as nausea, great weakness, a weak and rapid pulse, and a profuse flow of saliva. Muscular paralysis may occur in the untreated patient, and the individual may pass into a stupor.

Tissue loss may be great on hands or feet where bitten. Much depends on the size of the snake and the amount of venom injected. The time interval since the snake most recently struck and emptied his poison sacs also is a factor.

• *If You Have Ice—The Freezing Treatment*

These days many campers have ice, especially those who travel by boat or motor vehicle. The best procedure is to put a tight ligature (tourniquet or narrow binding) several inches above the bite on the side of the heart. Release briefly every five minutes until the extremity can be put into a fifty-fifty mixture of ice and water. Never use salt water.

Immerse well above the bite. In an ankle bite, for example, immerse to the knee; with a finger bite, immerse to elbow. Pain from both the bite and the cold will leave in about five minutes. With this mixture it is impossible to get the water temperature below 37° so there will be no danger of frostbite or freezing.

The tourniquet should be removed within three to five minutes after immersion, then kept off. After three or four hours of this treatment, pack the extremity with improvised ice bags. Plastic bags will do nicely.

If the patient is not sensitive to horse serum, as soon as possible inject one-half of an ampule of antivenin at the site of the bite and the other half at a higher level in the same extremity. Complete instructions come with the antivenin kit, detailing how to mix it, how to test for allergy, and how to use it. Incidentally, go ahead with the recommended skin test on an uninvolved part of the body, but get the affected part immediately in ice. If the allergy test is negative, proceed with the antivenin.

When you are in snake country, it is a good idea to carry one venom kit and a set of suction cups, which will be discussed below. To each person given more than one ampule of antivenin, a serum reaction can develop in two to five days which may prove more of a problem than the bite. This also is discussed fully in the instruction book that comes with the kit. The kit can be procured through any drug store. Because of the tendency for reactions with added ampules of antivenin, many doctors use no more than one ampule, as outlined above.

A tetanus shot should be given if the individual has not had a booster recently, and it will be well to start penicillin or another antibiotic. Erythromycin 250 mg. four times daily for four to seven days is a good choice, depending on the general condition of the patient.

After twenty-four to thirty-six hours, allow the extremity to warm slowly. Swelling will occur and last for several days, but it will be far less than with other methods of treatment.

If treatment is delayed one or two hours, it is not as effective, although it still will be better than nothing. On most bites small, distended, dome-shaped blisters and blue discoloration occur in the area of the bite, and later the tissue sloughs off. Often the extremity is numb for two or three years afterward. This is due to the venom, not the cold treatment.

Immediately after the bite, exertion is to be avoided, also coffee and alcohol. The person bitten should be kept lying down and quiet to slow his circulation and retard absorption of the poison. This is the ideal. Anything less is more hazardous.

• *Treating With Suction Cups*

Snakebite kits, which take up little more room in the pocket than a 12-gauge shotgun shell, are widely available. Their function is based on suction cups.

Keep as quiet and calm as possible, thereby avoiding to the greatest possible degree any unnecessary quickening of the circulation which would speed absorption of the poison into the system. Drink no liquor or stimulants.

On extremities, tie a band one and one-half inches above both bite and swelling, if possible, to restrict the flow of the lymph vessels only, not the veins. A handkerchief, tie, torn strip of clothing, or lace, will serve. *It must not be tight!* This is *not a tourniquet,* nor should one be applied in this particular treatment. Loosen a bit if the limb numbs or becomes cold. Remove the band for a minute about once every ten minutes. Continue, if you can, to apply slightly higher, so it will be just beyond the extending swelling.

Clean the skin as well as possible where any cutting is to be done, so as not to complicate the situation by introducing germs or dirt into these wounds. Paint with antiseptic if any is available, or wash with detergent or soap if this can be done with a minimum of delay.

If antiseptic is not available with which to paint the knife blade, sterilize it in a fire or over a match flame. Then make a quarter-inch cut to or slightly below the depth of the bite through each fang mark.

During all the cutting, be extremely careful to avoid arteries, tendons, nerves, and large veins. Do not make incisions if the bite is over visibly prominent veins.

Squeeze air out of the suction cup and place over the cuts. Steady, gentle suction is preferable to strong suction, so don't pump. The cup will hold better if the skin is first moistened. Additional incisions are made and the cup applied as the swelling progresses. Full directions come with the suction cups.

Lacking a suction pump or cups, suck and spit out blood and venom. A warmed bottle will, as it cools, also provide suction. If you can do nothing better, perhaps because of the position of the bite, press and squeeze out blood and venom.

Then proceed with antivenin as suggested in the preceding treatment. Again, a tetanus shot should be given if the patient has not had a booster recently, and it will be advisable to start penicillin or another antibiotic, such as 250 mg. of Erythromycin four times a day for four to seven days.

### • Serum Reaction

Snake antivenin is made by injecting the venom into horses until they produce an immunity (antibodies) to it. This serum then is used to transfer the resistance temporarily to the person bitten.

A serum reaction is a delayed reaction, occurring in from two to four or five days in an individual sensitive to antivenin. It is manifested by temperature, swollen arthritic-type joints, and other symptoms causing misery. The reaction is treated with bed rest and with antihistaminics (Pyribenzamine, in doses of 50 mg. each four hours, four times daily being a good one), aspirin, and, under a doctor's care, cortisone.

For one bitten by a poisonous snake, one could well risk one vial of serum, but each succeeding vial increases the likelihood of a reaction.

● *Ticks*

Ticks attach themselves to the body and become engorged with blood before dropping off. They pass on a group of diseases, mostly in the Rocky Mountain belt. The longer the infected tick is attached, the more it regurgitates the virus into the host, and the greater the chance of the individual's becoming ill. It is suggested that all in the Rocky Mountain area be immunized for Rocky Mountain Spotted Fever before going afield.

Tick removal is a delicate matter, but in any event inspection for the pests at least three times daily in tick country is a good idea. Sometimes holding a heated object near the tick, or dabbing on grease or kerosene or gasoline, will cause it to withdraw, but don't count on it. On the other hand, be very careful how you pull it off or the head will be left in to cause infection. Another problem with pulling off the tick is that the infected, gorged blood in the tick is inoculated back into the host.

You can use an 11 Bard-Parker scalpel blade, the one also employed for snakebite incisions, and dig the head out by lifting the tick upwards to arch its back, so to speak, and working around the head from the back forward.

● *Black Widow Spider*

This bite is much overrated and is rarely fatal in healthy individuals. The Black Widow is a glossy, moderately large, black spider. Fine body hairs give it a silky appearance. On the underside of the abdomen is a characteristic reddish marking in the form of an hourglass. Only the female is poisonous. The much smaller male is harmless.

A bite causes local swelling and redness. This is the only reaction that may occur in many, but in some severe muscular cramps and pain may ensue. Nausea, vomiting, and a shock-like state also may occur. Recovery is the rule. The exception to this is a bite on the penis. The Black Widows often will inhabit the underside of outhouse seats, where they capture flies and where the unsuspecting may sit. In event of such bite, the sufferer should be evacuated to where professional help is available.

Otherwise, the treatment of Black Widow bites is largely a supportive one. Darvon Compound or aspirin is used for the pain and cramps. Cold compresses applied to the site of the bite help reduce swelling and delay absorption of the venom. In a hospital, injections of calcium are effective in counteracting the effect of the bite, but in the bush this probably is not necessary because recovery is the rule.

- *Brown Spider Bite*

This is mentioned for the sake of completeness and because a bite from this critter can cause a painful ulcer to form. After the bite, the skin in the immediate area becomes gangrenous (dead), and after a week or so it will slough off. An ulcer remains which may take several weeks to heal. All the time this is going on, it hurts like blazes.

The area is best covered lightly and kept covered with Baciguent ointment to minimize infection. The Brown Spider is common in the West and Southwest.

- *Sensitivity to Insect Bites*

This can be serious, indeed. More people die from insect bites each year than from snakebite. Within a few minutes after the sting of a bee or wasp, by far the most common offenders, the sensitive individual gets light-headed, faint, and his skin cool and moist. There may be shortness of breath, then shock and loss of consciousness.

Treat for shock. Never give the bitten person anything by mouth unless he is awake. An antihistaminic helps. (Also, see Cortisone.) Those sensitive can get a special kit, with adrenalin and all the necessary items in it, from their doctor. They should be completely familiar with its use—a topic involving instruction beyond the scope of this book.

All insect bites pose the problem of tetanus and infection. Itching can be lessened with a starch paste or starch bath as already described in the chapter on skin infections, and by a regular dose of aspirin. The infection from bites usually occurs from the bite itself, and not so much from the itching. If an infection should occur, the use of an antibiotic would be indicated.

Limbs, in particular, sometimes become badly swollen by multiple fly and mosquito bites. This can be handled with cool starch baths, aspirin by mouth, and Pyribenzamine, one 50-mg. tablet each four hours for the allergic component. Pyribenzamine also is valuable for counteracting bee bites and other insect bites.

### • *Rabies and Animal Bites*

The three problems with any bite, aside from tissue damage, are tetanus, infection, and rabies. Fortunately, rabies is rare, but it is 100 percent fatal if it develops. A person cannot be immunized against rabies before he is bitten, but to save his life he must surely be given correct professional treatment after such a bite.

First, it is important to capture and kill the wild animal which did the biting, if at all possible. The animal's head should be kept on ice until examined by a specially trained person, usually someone from a health department, to determine whether or not rabies actually is present. This refers, of course, to the more conventional circumstances and may be a procedure impracticable in the bush.

The decision to be made involves grave difficulty: If bitten by a genuinely rabid animal, the person not given skilled medical treatment will become a fatality. When it really is not a rabies case, there is a chance of fatality if the case is treated as though it were. Hence the need is underscored for positive findings whether the animal actually was rabid, a paramount consideration before proceeding with treatment of the bite.

The proper treatment of a rabies bite, incidentally, involves a daily injection for twenty-one days. While the risks attending such treatment are not ones to be taken lightly, they are nevertheless preferable to the overwhelming odds of a fatality if the bite truly represents a rabies case and escapes correct medical treatment.

For bites on the extremities and torso, a delay of a week can occur before treatments begin. For face and neck bites, treatment should be started immediately. This means evacuation of the patient.

There is no problem, of course, if one is bitten by a dog that has been immunized against rabies. The custom is to keep both immunized and non-immunized dogs physically restricted for ten days. Restriction means just that. The dog must not be able to run loose nor escape unless you wish to go through the agonizing dilemma of deciding whether or not to use the rabies-shot treatment series.

If the dog remains well (cats, too) during this

restrictive period, then rabies is ruled out. If the dog dies, then he may or may not have had rabies, and his brain must be examined by a specialist, as described. A stray animal that escapes after causing a bite always is a problem. It is customary to treat for rabies in such a case.

What about bites on the face and neck from an apparently well, but non-immunized dog? The procedure is to confine the dog and start the rabies treatments, but to discontinue the treatments if the animal remains well after his confinement period.

To sum it up, where rabies could be involved, seek professional medical help *at once!*

## 17

---

# THE LIGHTWEIGHT KIT—
# FOR SHORT TRIPS

A DOCTOR is interested in the proper handling of any medical problems he is likely to encounter on an outing. If he also likes to backpack, he is concerned with reducing the weight of necessary supplies to an absolute minimum. This chapter describes a medical kit that can be used to treat everything from a case of dysentery to a laceration. It weighs less than four ounces.

The items selected by the physician-outdoorsman for such kits are not what the average fellow would carry. This is an important point. The average outdoorsman carries a lot of worthless bulk, and nine times out of ten he does the wrong thing with what he does have. If a fellow is going to the trouble of carrying a medical kit, then he should have an effective one. There are literally thousands of drugs on the market, and yet years of experience have proved that the mere handful next discussed are the most essential.

While the contents suggested are not as readily procurable as those of the conventional type, they are well worth the effort of acquiring. You'll need prescriptions from your doctor, and you can get the supplies from your druggist or a surgical supply house.

Don't let some of the jaw-breaking names discourage you. Copy them down or, better, take this book with you when you ask your doctor for the needed prescriptions. You should see him, in any event, for a complete physical examination if you contemplate an extended trip in the wilderness. Besides, one or more of the suggested items may be replaced by something better on the market by the time you're ready to go. Too, your physician may be able to suggest something manufactured under another name by a different pharmaceutical house that will save you money.

There are very few effective drugs available without a prescription anymore because of Federal laws governing the sale of drugs over-the-counter. Getting a prescription, or having one called in to the drug store, should present no problems, however, if you get in touch with your physician and explain what you want and how you desire to use it. Most doctors would be happy to oblige if they knew the drugs would not be used indiscriminately. Your physician may even give you some of them at no cost from samples which he constantly receives.

An effort has been made to use only medications which are in a dry form so spillage and freezing will not be a problem. There are hundreds of drugs from which to choose, but an attempt has been made to select those which have the broadest possible coverage and the least number of untoward reactions.

Some compromise has been necessary in avoiding liquids. For example, it is less preferable to use an ointment in the eye if there is a corneal abrasion. A liquid with the same ingredients is better. Nevertheless, the ointment is more convenient to carry and can be safely used, so it is recommended.

The total cost of this short-stay or backpacking trip kit should not be more than eighteen to twenty dollars. This may seem expensive but when you consider that a simple hunting or fishing trip today can cost much more than this just for travel and other expenses, the kit cost is not out of line and the kit can be carried on many trips, not just one.

● *Antibiotics*

Erythromycin is suggested as the antibiotic of choice. Very few people are allergic to it, and the drug covers a wide range of infections. In some infections, penicillin or other antibiotics might work better. But if only one antibiotic is to be carried, then the Erythromycin probably is the best one.

In general, an antibiotic should be given until the individual is well and all signs of fever and infection have ceased. As with a fire, you have to keep putting water on the trouble, and you can't stop. The *worst thing* ever to do is to take an antibiotic now and then as the symptoms manifest themselves. If started, the antibiotic *must* be taken every four hours four times daily, never missing a dose, for a minimum of three days.

● *Allergy*

If an allergy to a medicine is suspected, such as hives or vomiting, stop the medicine. Allergy problems are not always easy to determine. All aspects must be weighed. Certainly, if you were treating pneumonia, you would think twice before stopping an antibiotic. On the other hand, treatment of a toothache could be more safely neglected. Sometimes, simply changing the dosage schedule and taking the prescription after or with meals may make the difference between success and failure. In some people an antibiotic may cause nausea, yet the medication can safely be continued.

● *Ointments*

With ointments, remember that if some is good, more is *not* better. You can't do more than cover the area. Covering it with a thick layer is no better than a thin layer. This also applies to eye ointments.

## • Cleansing

Note that in these listings Merthiolate and iodine are conspicuous by their absence. Soap and water should be used to clean wounds. Merthiolate, iodine, and other such antiseptics do more damage than good.

## • Obtaining the Drugs

Unless these drugs can be scrounged from a friendly physician's samples, as they often can be, it is to be noted that in most states there is a minimum prescription fee. Thus a prescription for ten Darvon Compound tablets would cost the same as a prescription for twenty. If the druggist is only labeling these bottles according to contents, however, he may make an exception to this rule. Ask him.

If your physician knows that these drugs are to be taken only when you are away from any available medical care, he probably will agree to let you have them. Basically, he is responsible for the use of any drug he prescribes. Research from day to day changes things. If he disapproves of a drug suggested, or if that drug has been discontinued, follow his advice. Ultimately, he knows your particular needs better than do the writers.

● *Morphine and Pain-Relieving Drugs*

Morphine is a good drug. If your physician approves, he can procure it for you in a disposable syringe and show you how to use it. In most instances, however, the codeine or Darvon Compound is more readily available and will suffice.

Incidentally, many people can't take codeine. It causes cramps and vomiting in some. Darvon Compound, which is not as effective, has few side effects and may be helpful for those who can't take codeine.

Aspirin, too, is a very useful drug. It works on pain from muscles and skin. Although it will not help with intestinal pain or urinary discomfort, it works for headache, itching, sunburn, and other burns, eye irritation, and ear pain. It reduces fever, and also works for joint and bone pain, toothache, and soreness of throat.

● *Cortisone*

Although valuable as an adjunct to therapy, cortisone ordinarily is not used. Its role is to depress inflammation, and it will cause remarkable amelioration of symptoms when standard methods fail. It must never be used if the patient has a history of tuberculosis or stomach ulcer.

Cortisone causes inflammation, not infection, to be suppressed. It is useful in the following: shock,

[ 163 ]

bursitis, allergic reactions with hives—as after bites from wasps and other pests, tenosynovitis, and poison oak or poison ivy. This prescription would be used for severe hives that followed an insect bite and that did not respond after twenty-four to forty-eight hours to standard treatment. It is of value if serum sickness should follow the use of antivenin in snakebite; a prescription of thirty tablets should see one through such a crisis. In shock, this drug can be life-saving.

It is best carried in the form of Prednisone, the 5-mg. size. Take one tablet each four hours four times daily for four days. Then taper to one tablet each twelve hours for two days. It always is necessary to taper the dose.

## • Weight

The medicine kit for a short trip of a week, for example, weighs less than four ounces. This does not include the snakebite suction cups and the antivenin.

The items in the short kit and in the long kit (next chapter) can vary according to need. Thus those who are highly allergic may want cortisone (Prednisone) in their short kit, although ordinarily one would not carry this item unless he were to be away from civilization for more than a week.

Amounts of drugs also would vary, of course, on a longer trip. Although a dozen antibiotic tablets

(Erythromycin) probably would do for a short trip, you might want thirty-six tablets for a longer stay.

● *Contents of Short-Stay or Backpacking Trip Kit*

A.P.C. (same as EMPIRIN)—5-grain tablets. Dose: two each four hours. Indications: headaches, particularly at high altitudes.

ASPIRIN—5-grain tablets. Take two each four hours. For headaches, burns, joint or muscle pain, earache, toothache, sore throat, sunburn, etc. Of no use for stomach pains. Reduces fever, however. Over ten tablets daily may cause ringing in the ears. Also may irritate stomach. If so, take with food.

*A dozen tablets of either should suffice*

ASPIRIN WITH CODEINE—Half-grain codeine capsules. One each three to four hours for severe pain or discomfort. Codeine also controls a cough. There are a few side effects of stomach cramps and vomiting in sensitive people.

*Six tablets are adequate for short stay*

DARVON COMPOUND—One-grain. This compound is an alternative to codeine. There are less side effects in many people, although it is not as potent as co-

deine, nor does it have the cough-suppressing effect
that codeine has.

*Can substitute for the aspirin with codeine
No need for both on a short trip*

COMPAZINE—Five-mg. tablets. One each four
hours for nausea or vomiting. There may be some
drowsiness with continued use.

*Four to six tablets enough*

PROBANTHINE—For stomach spasms or diarrhea
cramps. One each four hours. Causes dryness of
mouth, some trouble focusing on fine objects, and
in some people, hesitancy of urination.

*Six to eight tablets*

LOMOTIL—For diarrhea. Take one or two tablets
each three to four hours until diarrhea is under control, then one each four hours.

*Carry twelve tablets*

PYRIBENZAMINE—50-mg. tablets. One each four
hours. To be used to dry up a cold, for sniffles, itching eyes where dust or allergy might be a factor,
hives, insect bites, and in other conditions where
allergy may be a factor. Hence, we would use it in

serum sickness or to prevent it if antivenin is used, in poison ivy, and other contact phenomena of the skin, and itching in general.

*Carry six tablets*

BISMUTH AND PAREGORIC—Not suitable for short-stay or hiker's kit because of weight. (See next chapter.)

SULFASUXIDINE—.5-gm. tablets. Usually, take two or three each four hours for dysentery, if there is fever and it does not respond to simple measures. Idiosyncrasies to intestinal sulfa are rare, but care should be taken with those who have a history of sulfa-allergy.

*Carry sixteen*

PYRIDIUM AND GANTRISIN—see next chapter.
Optional in short kits. Advisable if women, or people who have a history of urinary tract infection or problems, are along.

*Six to eight Pyridium tablets and
thirty-six Gantrisin tablets*

ERYTHROMYCIN—250-mg. tablets. Use for infection, one each four hours at meals and bedtime. Use three or four days ordinarily, but longer for tonsillitis, pneumonia, and certain other special cases mentioned in text. May cause heartburn if not taken with meals, as well as loose stools in a few. Expiration date in two or three years. Check with druggist as to when supply should be replaced.

### Twelve for short stay

DEXEDRINE—Five-mg. tablet. For energy. Not recommended except in an emergency. Then take one every four to six hours.

BUTYN, OR METYCAINE AND MERTHIOLATE— These eye anaesthetics all are ointments. After use, take care to protect eye against further injury and from foreign bodies, as their entry will not be detected when the eye is anaesthetized. Use for foreign body in eye, snow blindness, etc.

### Two or three

PONTOCAINE—This eye anaesthetic is a liquid and, therefore, is not so easily handled on a short trip. Its effect is more predictable, however. Use Ophthalmic Pontocaine, ¼ % only.

SPECTROCIN EYE OINTMENT—For eye infection. This also can be used in ear for external otitis.

### Apply each four hours.

● *Surgical Supplies*

1. Roller gauze, 1 or 2 inch
2. Telfa (non-sticking gauze)
3. Small assorted adhesive bandages
4. 3 x 3 or 4 x 4 flats
5. Scalpel blades, 11 Bard-Parker and curved blade
6. Suture material, three-0 and five-0 nylon with needle attached in sterile packet
7. Mosquito clamp
8. Manicure scissors
9. Package of Butterflies for holding together wounds without suturing. Comes in three sizes.
10. Packet of three-0 plain catgut for ties on bleeders.
11. Oil of cloves for those with toothaches.

● *Snake Country*

Set of suction cups and antivenin kit. The latter expires in four to five years. Avoid excess heat and freezing. In between trips, follow storage instructions accompanying the container.

# 18

## THE LIGHTWEIGHT KIT
## EXPANDED—FOR LONGER TRIPS

THE FOLLOWING MEDICINE CHEST should be adequate for a longer stay, or when several people will be in the party. Double or triple the quantities of drugs suggested for the light kit. Otherwise, make up as follows.

ASPIRIN—100 tablets will be a good idea.

ASPIRIN WITH CODEINE—Twenty-four.

DARVON COMPOUND—Eighteen tablets in addition to the above codeine will be adequate.

COMPAZINE—Twelve.

LOMOTIL—Thirty-six.

SULFASUXIDINE—Fifty tablets for one individual, one hundred for several.

BISMUTH AND PAREGORIC—Eight ounces, mixed in equal parts.

PROBANTHINE—Thirty-six.

PYRIDIUM—Eighteen. Take one every four to six hours. If this causes stomach irritation, take with food, otherwise as needed. Pyridium will stop all urinary burning and distress. It will color the urine red.

GANTRISIN—Fifty. These are for treatment of a urinary tract infection, as well as for the continued treatment of strep infections, pneumonia, and the like. They can be used if only a few antibiotic tablets are carried, and the condition requires additional treatment. Some individuals are sensitive to sulfa. Gantrisin should be discontinued if there is rash, fever that comes and goes when the sulfa is used, or nausea or vomiting.

ERYTHROMYCIN—Twenty-four or thirty-six tablets, depending on the remoteness and the number of people.

PYRIBENZAMINE—Thirty-six.

DEXEDRINE—Twelve.

CORTISONE (PREDNISONE)—Thirty.

STERILE VASELINE—One tube.

BACIGUENT—One one-ounce tube of this antibiotic ointment should do.

ZINC OXIDE—One tube, for chapped lips or for mixing in equal parts with Eugenol to make a temporary filling for a tooth.

EUGENOL—One-quarter ounce bottle will be adequate.

OIL OF CLOVES—Small bottle, as only a few drops are needed for toothache.

For surgical supplies, it is suggested that you take both a two-inch and a four-inch Ace or similar elastic bandage. Although optional for a short trip, these are very handy for holding splints, etc.

The amount of gauze and tape to pack along is optional, particularly as it is always possible to improvise. For a long stay, two packs of each type of suture material are recommended.

You'll want a thermometer. Check this before taking a temperature and first shake its mercury down, if necessary. There is no absolute normal temperature. Ignore the red marks on the thermometer. They do not mean fever unless the temperature is over 99.6°. Keep the thermometer in a case and out of the sun. In most cases, a temperature taken under the tongue or armpit will suffice.

● *Costs*

Eighteen dollars should do it for the light kits, plus several dollars more for the snakebite kit with suction cups. Add eight to ten dollars for antivenin.

The cost of the long-stay chest will vary according to the amounts of medications, etc. taken. Generally, the price per tablet lowers as more tablets are bought. Your doctor may even be able to help you with some of the drugs he constantly receives as samples, and as pointed out, if the druggist simply labels drugs as to contents, he may be able to set up the kit for you at some saving.

Don't skimp on drugs. A lifetime of research has gone into them. There is absolutely no substitute for them when they are needed.

*Your life may depend on them.*